# Pre TEEN POWER

## A Treasury of Solid Gold Advice for Those Who Are Just Entering Their Teens

### from America's Top Youth Speakers, Trainers and Authors

Karl Anthony • Eric Chester • John Crudele
Phil Boyte • Jennifer Esperante Gunter • Norm Hull
Mike Patrick • Heather Schultz • Tony Schiller
Cami Veire • M. K. Durand Farley • Dennis Mitchell
and C. Kevin Wanzer

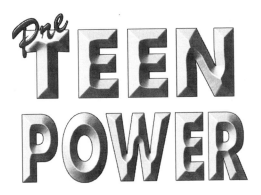

Compiled by
# Eric Chester

Printed by Patterson Printing, Benton Harbor, Michigan

Cover design and layout by Ad Graphics, Tulsa, Oklahoma
(800) 368-6196

Library of Congress Catalog Card Number: 97-065416

ISBN: 0-9651447-3-9

TEEN POWER™
TEEN POWER TOO™
PreTEEN POWER™
TEEN EmPOWER™
are registered trademarks of ChesPress Publications

Published by:

**ChesPress Publications**
a subsidiary of Chester Performance Systems
1410 Vance St., Suite 201
Lakewood, CO 80215
(303)239-9999

Additional copies of
PreTEEN POWER
can be obtained from any of the authors.
Contact information is at the end of the book.

Quantity discounts are available.

Web Site: www.teenpower.com

# Contents

## Where the authors are from, by chapter number

# Introduction

What are you doing? Can't you read? What does it say at the top of the page? Let's review, shall we? I-N-T-R-O-D-U-C-T-I-O-N. Do you know what that means? Look it up. It means – "Skip this part and go directly to the good stuff." What do you really expect in an introduction anyway? *"Hello, I am a book. Nice to meet you. And what is your name?"* You see, normal people don't read introductions.

Hmmm, but then again, maybe you are not normal.

Well, if that is the case, then you've come to the right book! Welcome my pre-teen friend. You are right where you need to be. What lies ahead is a wonderful collection of chapters assembled by the top "movers and shakers" when it comes to finding the power in people just like you. The stories that follow will make you laugh, cry, think, jump for joy, and maybe even take a few notes.

Well, maybe the note part is stretching it a bit....

One thing is for sure; you will not be the same when you are finished reading this book. So, pick a chapter – any chapter – and dive right in. The teenage years are right around the corner, and you're holding the road map that can help you get there in style. My fellow authors and I simply want you to enjoy the journey and demonstrate the courage to do what is right, regardless of the consequences.

After reading PreTeen Power, we hope that you no longer "fit in." (This world has enough "ins.") Our wish for you is that you go out into your teenage years and break the mold. And if it ain't broke – break it! You have the power; it is in your hands! Literally.

Happy reading!

Your POWERful friend,
C. Kevin Wanzer

# Who Really Cares

by
KARL ANTHONY

Pre
TEEN
POWER

# Who Really Cares

by

<u>KARL ANTHONY</u>

## The Sssssssss sound

I was a kid with a speech impediment. That just means I talked funny. Well, I should say other people thought it was funny. I didn't think so at all at the time. Every time I opened my mouth, all the sounds of each letter in the alphabet would come out perfectly except for the Sssssssss sound. No matter how hard I would try, I couldn't say the letter S. It was like my mouth forgot how to do it. Now trust me, when you can't say one of the letters in the alphabet like the letter S you tend to __ound kinda __tupid.

**But I knew I was not stupid**, even though, believe me I was reminded daily by other kids and even some so called friends, that I sounded that way.

I didn't always talk that way. It lasted for two solid years. You know two Summers, two Thanksgivings, two Christmas', two entire school years. It seemed like forever but it really wasn't.

I remember the first day it started. It was the morning after the big family announcement. My Dad had something he wanted to say to the whole family so he asked my brother and sisters and myself to sit down at the dining room table so he could speak with us all together. I figured we were in some kind of big trouble or something until I noticed my brother and sisters were looking pretty worried. It was like everybody knew what was going on except me.

Dad sat down at the head of the table, looked at all of us real serious and said, "**Tomorrow morning I won't be here. Your mother and I have decided to get a divorce.**"

Sure enough the morning came and he was gone, and believe it or not so were my S's. It was strange. I remember crying myself to sleep that night because it felt like my world was coming to an end. I was angry and sad at the same time about Mom and Dad splitting up but I refused to talk to anyone about my feelings. It turned out that I was only hurting myself because when I woke up the next morning and I tried to speak, I couldn't pronounce my S's. That is when the speech impediment started. Sometimes a painful experience can hurt you worse when you don't talk to someone about it.

## Ned The Neighbor

If that wasn't bad enough, shortly after my parents divorced and my S's went bye bye, something else extremely terrible happened. It was the end of summer and the first day of school was fast approaching. You won't believe what my mother said to me. She said,

**"Young man this year, before school begins, you <u>will</u> get a decent hair cut!"**

Now please, you have to understand it doesn't sound like much but this was years ago when long hair was the bomb and getting your hair cut…well…waaaay back then, especially before the first day of school, meant possibly looking like a total Dork; more than likely I would be alienating myself from any possible social interaction or for that matter any acceptance from my fellow classmates. So I pleaded with my mother to please have mercy on me, wouldn't she please reconsider. I would do anything, even clean my room…well…maybe not clean my room. It didn't matter what I promised her, she wouldn't budge. It was clear if I wanted to live, I was going to get an unnecessary haircut to a perfectly good head of hair.

My Mom always told me money was a little tight and getting a hair cut cost money, so to save a few dollars, she had a brilliant idea. It involved our neighbor.

His name was Ned…Ned The Neighbor.

Ned the neighbor used to fix things around the house occasionally and my Mother put great faith in his abilities. She had so much faith in him that one day she asked Ned the neighbor,

**"Pardon me Ned, I've noticed that your yard always looks so nice. Do you think that perhaps since you're so good**

at keeping your hedges so perfectly trimmed in your yard, that you might possibly be able to give my young Anthony here, a little trim?"

I watched Ned the neighbor instantly freeze with anticipation. Then ever so slowly he turned his neighborly head toward me glaring with his beady eyes as he scratched his chin.

I just knew he was remembering all the times when I rode my tricycle through his wife's flower garden or perhaps that unforgettable time I drained all the water out of their swimming pool in the middle of winter, in order to turn the neighborhood into a giant ice skating rink.

Whatever he was thinking about, Ned grinned at me with an evil kind of stare and responded to my Mom without hesitation;

*"Yeah...sure! No problem....I'll cut the kid's hair."*

I was doomed! Definitely toast! I knew I was dead meat because he offered to start that instant. He immediately grabbed the scissors and then he plopped me down on his riding mower in the garage, as he shouted to my Mom, "Don't worry, this one is on the house."

Mom was so happy to be getting such a great deal, but I on the other hand was terrified. Plus, I couldn't help but keep my mind on the fact that Ned the neighbor didn't have one hair on top of his head, not one! And as you can imagine when he was finished with me, **neither did I.**

…Oh don't get me wrong, I was happy he decided to leave both my ears intact and most of my facial features, but he didn't leave much of anything else, except for one little flip of hair in front sticking straight up from the top of my head. It went up and then it came down, dangling over my forehead and fell right between my eyes. It looked ridiculous…I swear I looked like a pheasant walking down the street! All I could think about was that first day of school. I didn't even want to take a step outside of my own house I felt so embarrassed.

## Everyone Has Feelings

Now think about it for a minute…if every time you opened your mouth to speak it sounded really bizarre and hardly anybody could understand you, and your hairstyle made you look like some kind of goofy bird, do you think you would be looking forward to the first day of school? **Not exactly!**

I didn't look forward to the second day, or the third day, or even the fourth day, or just about any day, that whole year.

That was the year I found out who really cared about me and I have to admit it wasn't as many people as I hoped. I guess kids would tease me so much because I was different than they were. I really think it was just that they didn't know how to act around people who were different. Have you ever met someone like that? I learned, everyone has feelings even though they might pretend they don't.

## Trust and the Bobbie Pin

There were some things my Mom used to tell me to do that I would obey without compromise. Like those unforgettable moments when she would ask me to sit down so she could clean my ears out. So what's the big deal? Well, it was how she went about it and of course the tool of choice she would use for the operation. That's right, she used a bobbie pin. *NO KIDDING!* She really would. Q-tips must not have had that scrapable edge she required. Mom would tell me, "Now be…veeerrry still because, *THIS IS DANGEROUS!*"

"**Dangerous!!**" I said. Then why was she sticking that thing in my ear anyway. Telling me it's dangerous must have been "**her special way**" of putting me at ease.

I would try to hold my breath while she was working on me, until she started making comments like "OH *MY! OH MY! WOULD YOU LOOK AT THAT!*"

I'm like…WHAT!…WHAT!…LOOK AT WHAT!

Out of the depths of my ear canal she would remove a huge glob of something disgusting with the help of her trusty bobbie pin and then she would stick it right in front of my face to say, "Look at what I found." I'm thinking, *NO!*......spare me the visuals.

Mom seemed so proud of it that she probably saved it to show her friends!

It would never fail that at the end of each ear cleaning experience my Mom would always tell me, now Karl, don't you ever let anyone else put a bobbie pin in your ears ......I'd say "UH OK." *Sometimes parents love to say what is completely obvious.*

You know, the truth is even as she was operating on my ears, I was never really that worried. I guarantee you I would never let anyone else come at me with a bobbie pin, especially to stick it in my ear, but with Mom it was different. Why? Because I knew I could trust her. I was positive beyond the shadow of a doubt she had my best interest at heart.

It sounds strange I know, but I knew that my Mom would never hurt me, not intentionally that is. Although, keep in mind, it is possible that someone can still hurt you even when they have good intentions. That is why it is important to always think. It's up to each and every person to decide for themselves who they can trust. Who are the people in your life that would never hurt you and that really care about you? As soon as you ask yourself that question, those individuals will come to mind.

**So how do you know when you can trust someone?** It's when you know beyond a shadow of a doubt, that someone absolutely has your best interest in mind. They care how **you** feel about things. They care about your opinions and listen to your suggestions. They never force you to do something you think isn't right even if they think it's okay.

Go ahead and trust someone when you are sure they really care about you. Until you know that, proceed with caution.

## One Nickel at a Time

Airports are the best place to watch people. I remember noticing a woman in the Dallas airport trying to ask for donations. She was collecting money for a local homeless shelter and I was amazed at how people were treating her. They were avoiding her as if she had green slime running down her face. I'm not kidding, people would go out of their way to ignore her. If that wasn't rude enough, some people would say cruel things. Keep in mind this woman was being very friendly as far as I could see. She wasn't being pushy or anything, she just simply said good morning as people walked by her and then she would give them a big smile announcing,

"Hello, I am collecting today for our local homeless shelter in the area to help those who are homeless get a fresh new start for themselves."

Sure, some people were more than happy to help out and there were even a few who said, "Oh I'm so sorry I can't give right now but I do appreciate what you're doing on behalf of the homeless." You could tell by the look in the woman's face that hearing that kind of comment made her feel just as good as if they had put ten dollars in the jar she had been holding all morning.

But then there were others who couldn't be satisfied with not contributing or just ignoring her, they would actually respond with rude and unkind comebacks like,

"Gave at the office…." "Tell them to get a job…." "I don't give to deadbeats…."

Most people would not even acknowledge her. One person actually held out a twenty and when she tried to receive it, he grabbed it back and laughed out loud…obviously showing off in front of his friends and acting like a total jerk.

After a little while, I walked up to her and gave her a small donation. She responded with a warm and friendly smile and quietly said,

"Thank you very much. We promise to put your contribution to good use at the homeless shelter."

I replied, "I'm certain you will and I am happy to be able to help out, but I'm curious about something. I notice that some people appear to care about others and some others don't seem to care about anything or anybody? I watched how people treated you today. Is it like that all the time? And if it is, it makes me wonder. Why do you think some people are so cruel?"

She paused for a brief moment before she replied, "The answer to that question is easy," she said, "They simply haven't learned compassion yet." "Compassion," I said. "How do you learn compassion?"

The woman said, "You learn compassion **one nickel at a time**" as she held up her donation jar and smiled. "Giving to others is the ultimate reward you give to yourself and the best way to learn." It doesn't have to be money, just giving to others is what matters. A smile or a kind word can make all the difference in a person's life, but what most people don't realize is that it helps the person who is giving the gift even more.

Then she told me, "I was once homeless and I lived on the streets. I know what it is like to need someone's help. The shelter that helped me is the one I am collecting contributions for now. I'm happy I have the opportunity to give back to those who gave to me. People from everywhere walk through this airport so I guess you can say I'm teaching the whole world a little compassion, **one nickel at a time**."

## The Last Word

Life is rich with experiences and I guarantee you will never run out of stories to tell about what you have gained from those experiences. I feel so fortunate to be able to tour all over the world doing what I love to do…playing music.

Traveling to so many different countries I have noticed that people everywhere care a lot about the same things…family, friends, education, home, music and maybe even themselves a little. It's important to take care of yourself as well as each other, then if you think about it, everyone is taken care of.

# Be Yourself – the Voices Scream

*What Does That Really Mean?*

by
PHIL BOYTE

# Be Yourself –
# the Voices Scream
## *What Does That Really Mean?*

by
### PHIL BOYTE

I t was hot! The muggy, sticky, heavy kind of hot when it hurts to breathe. On days like this the old man would leave his stuffy little home, come sit at the train station, and watch people. This particular day a young man with a small suitcase walked over, stooped to where the old man sat mopping his sweaty face with a rag and asked him a question.

"Excuse me sir, I am thinking about moving to this town. Could you tell me what kind of people live here?"

The old man stopped wiping his forehead, turned his stool and replied to the young man with a question of his own, "What kind of people lived in the town you are coming from?"

The young man quickly replied, "They were rude and mean and didn't care for other people very much, sir."

The old guy smiled, looked up at the young man and said, "Ya know, I think you'll find the people here just like that. Some mean and nasty and others who don't care much about anyone else."

"Thank you for your answer, sir," the young man replied, "I think I'll get back on the train and keep on going until I find a better town."

The old man scratched his head as the young man climbed back on the train and left town.

Time passes even in the heat when you're spitting seeds, swatting flies and wiping your face. Three hours passed and the afternoon train pulled into the station. The old man noticed another young man step off the train with a small suitcase, much like the young man who had left on the train a few hours before. This young man approached the old timer and stopped to ask a question.

"Sir, excuse me, but I have a question for you. I am thinking about getting off the train and moving into this town and I was wondering what the people here are like?"

The old man smiled and said, "Why don't ya tell me what the people in your last town were like."

The young man got a great big smile on his face and said, "They were the best! They were friendly and so nice. I had some great friends and hated to leave them, but I needed to move on so I could grow and experience new adventures."

The old man smiled and said, "I think you'll find the people here the very same as you did in the town you came from. They'll be nice and friendly and you'll make some great friends."

The young man said, "Thank you, sir," grabbed his bags and walked into town looking for a place to live.

The little lady selling candy at the counter nearby had been watching this old man for most of the day. "I don't understand," she cried, "You told the first man the people here were mean and nasty and yet you told the second young man that he would find great friends here. Why did you tell them different stories?"

The old man quietly said, "I didn't tell 'em anything about the people in this town. All I did was tell those boys they would find the people here the same as they did the people in the last town they were in. You see, we find in our town people who reflect what we are. If we are mean and nasty that is who we will find, but if we are friendly and kind then we'll find those people instead. It's who we are that makes the decision what kind of people we will find.

The old man sat back on his stool and continued to watch people as he wiped another drop of sweat from his head.

*What are people like at your school? How about in your neighborhood? We will find people just like us wherever we go. That is great for some of us and scary for others. What if you don't like who you are?*

My friend Derrick left Colorado and moved to a little village in Alaska to get away. Three months later he called and said, "I thought I would be a different person up here than I was in Colorado, but it's still the same old me. What can I do to change?"

*So many people want to give us the advice – **Be Yourself.** What does that mean? How do I "be myself" if I am trying to become who I want to be? What follows are several stories that helped people develop into who they wanted to be.*

## Carrie and Dennis

Our teacher was sitting on her desk crying when I walked into class on Wednesday. As I slipped into my desk I asked Jay what was going on. Under his breath he told me to SHUT UP! I had missed class the two days before because I was on a trip. When Mrs. Cohen finally started talking, it was in a soft and broken voice.

"I can't believe you kids. Why would you cheat on the test? You are smart kids and all but two of you cheated!"

She looked over at Dennis and said, "Dennis, you only missed two." Then she turned and looked at Carrie. Smiling through the tears she said, "Carrie, you got 100% without cheating. I am proud of you."

Carrie kind of smiled and looked down at her desk again. The rest of the kids were frozen in embarrassment. I was quietly glad I wasn't there the day of the test. The teacher went on with her speech while I sat and wondered if I would have cheated that day.

This happened in 1978 and I still remember it! The amazing thing is, I still remember Carrie and Dennis and I still remember they didn't cheat! One of the strongest memories I have from school is their honesty while all the other kids cheated. I would love to find Dennis and Carrie today and renew my friendship with them because I am sure that after twenty years, they are still honest.

*I want to have honest friends. I want to be around honest people. It is important to me because I am **becoming myself** and **myself** wants to be honest. Is it important to you? Are you honest? Does it really matter to be honest?*

Twenty years ago it mattered that Carrie and Dennis were honest. It mattered to the teacher then, and I realized how much I appreciated it later. The funny thing is I never told them I was glad they were honest that day. There are a lot of kids at your school that know you for who you really are and they appreciate the kids who are honest and nice. More important than me being glad they were honest, was Carrie and Dennis realizing their honesty was important to them. They learned something about who they were that day. They were "being themselves."

*Do you like who you are? When you are in a place to cheat what do you do? When it is over will you be glad with the choice you made? Are you "**being yourself** – the self you want to be?"*

## Mark

Mark is on my baseball team. He is twelve. Mark is a very good player so we asked him to pitch in an important game. He smiled, took the ball and strolled to the mound. After the first inning we were ahead 5-0. Mark pitched a great second inning and the other team still had no runs. After three innings he continued to pitch great and the score was 8-0. The fourth inning we moved Mark to shortstop. He made a great catch behind second base and was smiling real big when he came in to hit. It was the fifth inning where it all fell apart. At shortstop Mark made three mistakes. They weren't bad mistakes, just little things that helped the other team score runs and get extra bases. When our team came to the dugout after the inning Mark had tears streaming down his cheeks.

I called Mark to the side and asked him what was up. "Coach, I blew it. I made three mistakes and they scored seven runs against us," he cried.

We talked for a few minutes about how well he had pitched and about his earlier hit and how much he had helped the team. He walked back into the dugout without the tears. A minute later I heard a crash in the dugout. I looked in to see where Mark had thrown a bat at something and realized he was mad.

I called him aside and the tears came again. "Mark, when do you bat again?" I asked.

"Third," he mumbled.

"Mark, this team needs you now. If you go there to hit with these tears and thinking about your mistakes will you be a good hitter?" I asked.

"Probably not," he said quietly. "What do you have to do to hit well?" I continued to question.

"I have to concentrate on hitting and have a good attitude at the plate," was his reply.

"Mark, go get your bat and start thinking about hitting, and go up there with the attitude that you are going to get a great hit off this pitcher," I encouraged.

A few minutes later Mark went up to hit. I yelled, "Mark, let's see what you're made of!"

He smiled over at me and he hit the next pitch really far to left field. Running as hard as he could he slid into third base with a triple. When he stood up a huge smile came across his face.

*What are you made of? When things get hard do you want to quit? When you make a mistake do you want to give up?*

Mark realized that when he made a mistake he had to concentrate on what would make him successful and do that. On that Monday it worked, and Mark's triple scored two runs. Our team won the game. Some days it won't be a triple, but whatever the result, the important thing is after we make a mistake we go back to what we know makes us successful and do that until we do well again.

*This is how we decide who we are. Choosing not to give up when the going gets tough. Choosing to **be ourselves** by not quitting when every square inch of our body wants to.*

## Nate and Cody

Nate was always in trouble. The fifth grade teacher had to keep his eye on Nate all the time or Nate would be hitting someone and simply leave class to go wander down the hall. The kids in his class started to realize that Nate would go nuts if they simply teased him. They would call him names and chase him at recess. Sometimes they would whisper things in his ear during class just to see him explode and throw his books across the room. Then they would laugh when he got in trouble. Nate was always sitting in front of the principal's office.

Cody was different. He would play with Nate at recess and eat with Nate at lunch. When Nate would chase someone, Cody would grab him and hold him while telling him, "Nate, it's not worth the trouble." Cody was always trying to get kids to be friendly with Nate and quit the teasing. When I asked Cody what was going on with Nate he said, "It is really sad. His mom had cancer and when she died he came to live with his grandparents. He loved his grandma so much, and he and his grandpa did a lot of fun things together. He missed his mom but his grandma helped a lot. Then six months after he moved here his grandma died unexpectedly and Nate was really upset. After a few months he started getting better and then his grandpa came home with a new ladyfriend. Nate thought that was cool until he realized she might be his new grandma and then he just lost it again." Cody explained that Nate didn't want to get in trouble, but he was so upset with things that were happening at home he just got mad easy at school.

*Why are kids mean to other kids? Are they just **being themselves?** What made you tease the kid when you did it last? Was the kid fat or ugly or dirty or not very smart? Did you join other kids when they were doing it or did you start it?*

At Christmas time that year Nate brought Cody a gift to school, the only present he gave at school that year. Cody said, "I think I am the only friend Nate has. I think if other kids understood what Nate was going through they would be a lot nicer to him. Why do they have to be so mean?"

*What would have happened if the teasing had turned into words of encouragement for Nate? Choose to **be yourself** by standing alone against the others teasing, by sticking up for the Nates in this world. Choose to **be yourself** by listening to your heart.*

## Act As If

How do you become an honest person? The secret here is to **ACT AS IF** you are honest and you will develop that habit. When you have a choice to make, **ACT AS IF** you are honest and you will make the best decision. It is important that you have a reputation for being honest, but more important, is that you know in your heart you are an honest person like Carrie and Dennis. Then, when you are **being yourself**, you will be honest.

Do you want to be known as a person who comes back strong after making a mistake? The next time you make a mistake, **ACT AS IF** you come back strong and you will. More important than being known for that, is you knowing you will learn from your mistakes and come back strong like Mark did in his baseball game. Then, when you are **being yourself**, you will come back strong from mistakes and never give up when the situation gets tough.

Wouldn't it be great to treat those Nates in this world with respect? To play a part in helping them heal their broken hearts? The next time you are with one of those kids who are teased a lot, **ACT AS IF** you are the kind, thoughtful person who treats everyone with respect and you will treat the Nates at your school well. The best part is you will like yourself more. You will **be yourself**, the kind, generous human being that lives inside of you.

Hey, I hear a train pulling into the station, and look, I see a person getting off. Could it be you? I see you going over to that same, dripping with sweat, old man. You already know what he is going to answer when you ask him the question about the people in this place. What are you going to tell him? I think you will learn a lot about yourself when you answer his question. Yes, it is important to **be yourself**, and now you know a little of what it takes to **be yourself**.

*Remember, you've got to **ACT AS IF** you are the person you want to **BE**, and you will become just that, **YOURSELF!***

# We All Get Older...
## *But Not Everyone Grows Up!*

by
ERIC CHESTER

# We All Get Older...
## *But Not Everyone Grows Up!*

by

ERIC CHESTER

H ere I go again.... I'm just sitting here being weird.

For example, I've been curious about some things. If peanut oil comes from peanuts and vegetable oil comes from vegetables, where does baby oil come from? And why do women always open their mouths when they put on their eye makeup? If a tornado accidentally turned upside down, would it suck all the clouds down to earth?

Here's another weird idea for you. I'm going to purposely misspell the word "word": WERD. Now, try spelling it like that on a homework assignment. When your teacher circles it because it's misspelled, whip out this book, point to it, and demand to speak to your attorney.

Perhaps I'll call Dominoes, order a large pizza with no toppings, and ask them to "hold the crust." When they ask me where I live, I'll give them the address of the nearest Pizza Hut.

Eight bald men went to an Australian shoe farm to squeeze a roll of ketchup bottles while they sang a poem about Mount Kilfooey's banjo-playing soccer team. Sorry. I just felt compelled to write a sentence that no one has ever written before. Whew! Thanks, that felt great.

Pretty weird? Yep. Am I weird? Absolutely. And I don't mind admitting it.

Why? Because I'm not the average 40-year-old. I guess you could say that I was the type of kid who never wanted to grow "all the way" up. A part of me wasn't ready for advanced teenage life. Sure, I wanted to do the cool stuff that the older kids got to do: drive, stay up late, date, vote, and eat waffles. (Oh, I forgot. I could eat waffles. Sorry.) But I wanted no part of some of the stuff they had to do: work during the summer, pay taxes, get zits, and take Chemistry.

So there I was. Stuck in the middle. Longing for the advantages of being older, but not quite ready for the awesome responsibilities. Loving the freedom that came with childhood, but not wanting to be *treated* like a child. Hoping to be showered with toys at Christmas, but feeling too old to sit on Santa's lap. Being stuck right smack dab in the middle was pure torture!

Have you ever felt like that – stuck in the middle? If you have, trust me – the feeling passes. Someday, before you know it, you will get to drive, stay up late, date, vote, and eat waffles. (Oops! You can eat waffles now. Sorry.) And someday, my guess is that you'll also have to work, pay taxes, pop zits, and take Chemistry. Certainly, you will get older. But the big question is: *will you grow up*?

Not everybody does, you know.

I see older people doing "little people stuff" all the time. Stuff they shouldn't do. Stuff they know they shouldn't do. Stuff *you* wouldn't even do because you know better. Some older people never grew up; some kids never grow up. And that's a shame.

Now before I go on, let me explain the irony here. I've already told you that I was the kind of kid who never wanted to grow "all the way" up. I still don't. I love those times when I can think like a kid and feel like a kid. Thank God I have a wife who lets me be a kid every once in a while and kids who need an extra playmate. I'm especially grateful that I have a job that lets me work with kids of all ages and allows me to visit hundreds of schools every year. However, I know that I really am a grown adult. I have responsibilities, a job, and a full adult life.

So it comes down to this: you will get older, whether you like it or not. Age is something that just happens to you. But growing up is up to you. You won't hit a magical "birthday" that will suddenly make you a grown-up. Maturity is not about your age. Maturity is about your *ability* to make important choices that affect your life and then deal with the *consequences* of those choices.

We all want to make our own choices. Right now, you undoubtedly want to choose your own friends, your own clothes, your own classes, and your own bedtime. Some things you can choose; some things others choose for you. But you may not be completely ready to accept the results (or consequences) of those choices, especially if they are cruel or harsh. That's why parents and teachers give you *guidance*. They've experienced the road ahead of you. They want to help you avoid the pitfalls they *know* are there. So they influence and direct many of your choices to protect you from the tough consequences.

With all this in mind, I'd like to share some principles that will help you make better choices and avoid some of the pitfalls of growing up.

## Actions = Results

I'd love to take credit for inventing this principle, but it's been around since God was a little boy. The longer you live, the more experiences you will have. The more experiences you have, the more capable you will be in making bigger choices that greatly impact your life. Heck, you do things now that you couldn't have done two years ago! Two years from now, you'll be doing things you're not doing currently. You'll have more privileges but also more responsibilities. As you grow and experience life, you'll hopefully discover that your actions equal your results. Then you'll put more thought and care into your decisions and learn and grow as a result.

Sadly, some people act as if the "Action=Results" law doesn't apply to them. If they don't like the result (consequence) of an action (choice) that they've taken, instead of learning from their mistake (accepting responsibility) and changing their behavior, they repeat the action and again suffer the same result.

## A Loser's Game

What happens to a person after they've experienced a bad result from one of their actions? Perhaps they'll start playing "the blame game." You know the scene. . . a person had something go wrong or got into some sort of trouble. Now that person is looking to point the finger at someone else. *"Don't look at me – it wasn't my fault!" "The coach doesn't like me," "The teacher didn't go over that," "My parents didn't tell me," "He hit me first,"* or *"She was talking about me behind my back."* Kids aren't the only ones who make these childish remarks and demonstrate this childlike behavior. Older people who are not grown up say these things as well.

When Mike Tyson fought Evander Holyfield for the Heavyweight Boxing Championship, he feared he was losing and turned to cheating. You may remember what he did. He actually bit off part of Holyfield's ear! (Yuck!!! Didn't he eat dinner before the fight?) Sports fans (and for that matter, the entire world) thought Tyson's conduct was completely outrageous. But when asked about it, Tyson initially defended his actions, blaming his opponent for head-butting him. By trying to point the finger in Holyfield's direction, Mike Tyson lost millions of fans. Even though he later admitted he was indeed totally wrong, he wound up a big loser in the "blame game." **You must take responsibility for the consequences of your actions.**

## "Own Up" To Your "Goof Ups"

Face it – we all make mistakes. We all "goof up" now and then. Occasionally, we do stuff that is downright stupid. (That's okay. Only people who breathe make stupid mistakes.) It's what you do *after* you "goof up" that really determines whether you'll be successful in the future and whether you're mature or still a child.

For example, last summer my wife and I took our three kids – Travis, age 14; Zac, age 13; and Whitney, age 11 – on a trip to DisneyWorld. We were all "psyched" about it, and I did most of the planning. The morning of our vacation, Grandpa drove us to the airport. We arrived in plenty of time for our flight, which left at 10:30 a.m. With 45 minutes to spare, we went to a restaurant in the airport to relax before our flight. At 10:12, my son suggested that we head towards our gate. I checked the tickets for the departure gate number. As I read them, my jaw hit the floor. I couldn't believe my eyes! The flight time was actually 10:10, not 10:30 as I had thought. So there we stood in the airport jetway watching our plane pull away. We weren't on it, and it was all my fault! I wanted to scream. I wanted to cry. I felt horrible. I wanted to blame the airline, the person who checked us in, or the Governor of the State of Kalabooboo. But the fact of the matter was, I goofed!

At that point, I gathered my family around me and explained that I had read the departure time incorrectly. I told them how sorry I was. They all handled it like champs and quickly forgave me (even though they razzed me about it). We made the best of it and spent the first day of our vacation playing in the airport, waiting for the next available flight (which, incidentally, didn't get us to Orlando until 10:30 that evening)!

## Does "Owning Up" Get Us Out Of Trouble?

As a parent, I want my kids to admit when they were wrong or made a mistake. So I have to do what I expect them to do. "Owning up" is the first step in changing the attitude and behavior that led to the mistake in the first place. Then hopefully we won't make the same mistake again.

Travis, our oldest son, knew that we did not approve of his friend Mark. We encourage Travis to hang with kids who stay out of trouble, but Mark is the one kid in our neighborhood who always seems to find it. One night, Travis told us he was going over to Aaron's house to spend the night. The next morning, I called Aaron's to tell Travis something and his mom answered the phone. She told me that Aaron had stayed at his grandma's house the night before, and she hadn't seen Travis for a couple of days. When Travis came home, he admitted he lied and had actually spent the night at Mark's. He said that he didn't want to tell us the truth about where he was staying because he was afraid we wouldn't let him go. Since he was now being honest and "owning up," Travis thought that we would let him off without a punishment. He was unpleasantly surprised.

Admitting your mistakes does not make the consequences of your actions go away. If this were the case, you could rob a bank, buy some cool stuff, call the police, admit that you pulled the job, and go free. Nope. Admitting your mistakes helps you to learn and grow stronger, **but you can't escape the consequences of your actions.** That's why you need to carefully consider your choices and *think* before you act.

Case in point. When my daughter Whitney's cat, Cotton, licked Whitney's red hot curling iron, she learned a painful lesson real fast! As a result, Cotton never again went near the curling iron. In fact, Cotton never again went into that bathroom. If you licked a hot curling iron (which I don't suggest), you'd quickly learn a lesson too. The difference here between you and Cotton is that you'd apply what you learned to many different areas of your life. Even though you wouldn't let this experience prevent you from using the bathroom again, you'd probably think hard before you did anything even remotely related to it again. You'd definitely refrain from licking small electric appliances, especially if they were plugged in. The consequence (a sore tongue) would be around a while to serve as a friendly reminder.

## The Great News Is Found In 10 Two-Letter Words

So you're probably thinking, *"Dang, this chapter all of a sudden sounds like a lecture from my parents!"* I know, I know. But stay with me – this responsibility thing actually works in your favor.

Consider the power of these 10 two-letter words: **"IF IT IS TO BE, IT IS UP TO ME!"**

You are the one responsible for your actions. You are the one who must live with the results. You don't have to be Einstein to understand that if BAD ACTIONS=BAD RESULTS (Tyson's ear munching), then GOOD ACTIONS=GOOD RESULTS!

Let's say you have a math test tomorrow. (Don't freak; it's just an example!) And let's say that math is a difficult subject for you. Now imagine if tonight you studied two times harder than you normally do. Naturally, your grade would be higher than it otherwise would have been. Your good action (increased study) would create a good result (higher grade). The good result might even begin to multiply itself, leading to even more good results. (Higher math grade=happier mom. Happier mom=pizza for dinner instead of cabbage surprise casserole.)

Simply put, if you make good choices and follow up with good actions, good things will happen to you! There's no way around it! After all, you are in control, and your life is indeed "up to you!" Determine whether you want good results or bad results (duh) then take the correct action.

Yeah, you're going to goof up (make mistakes). Unfortunately, you'll sometimes suffer bad times even when you don't deserve it. The world has a strange way of challenging us. But remember – *you have your hands on the wheel of your life*. Once you understand the awesome power you possess, you'll assume the responsibility for making good choices and dealing with the consequences of your actions. In addition, you'll better handle the struggles that come your way through no fault of your own.

## So Go Ahead – Eat All The Waffles You Want!

Hey, don't be overly concerned about getting older faster so you can do more stuff, because those things will happen soon enough. Instead, enjoy the advantages of your current age. As you travel the road ahead, concentrate on growing and learning from the mistakes you make. Take responsibility for the results of your actions. Listen carefully to the advice of more experienced travelers (e.g., teachers, parents). Don't play the "blame game" or bite any ears. And whatever you do, if you see a red hot curling iron on the bathroom counter, don't lick it!

# Chapter 4

# Stand for Something…
# *or Fall for Anything*

by
JOHN CRUDELE

# Stand for Something...
## or Fall for Anything

by
JOHN CRUDELE

When I speak in elementary schools kids sit with their buns stuck to the floor like suction cups. They look up and shout, "I promise...I'll never use chemicals!" Elementary kids pledge to say "no."

I exclaim, "Who knows somebody who drinks?" And hands raise.

"My brother does," one kid shares. "He tries to get me to take a drink. That way, if I tell on him, he'll tell on me. But I say 'no!'"

Unlike elementary-age children, junior high school students are much more anxious about what others are doing. Girls form clicks, guys clumps. They look around wondering, "How do I fit in...with everybody?" We guys in junior high, we walk into the locker room, look down and notice seven hairs on our chest. Meanwhile, our buddy looks like a shag-carpet sample. Some think, "What's wrong with me? I'm falling behind, and I'm just getting started. I mean, my jock strap fits on both ways. Help!!!"

Girls are looking down and asking mom, "Why does one breast grow faster than the other? Come on, catch up, catch up! Oh no, I'm going to be lopsided! Ahhhhhh!!!"

Beyond the normal biological changes, other unexpected stresses may visit you. It's tough, for instance, when a family moves and throws kids into new neighborhoods, schools and friendships. Divorce also introduces different situations with fresh concerns. In either case, there's lots with which to deal.

I've met thousands of young people who, in the midst of this type of turmoil, desperately need to know they're important. One student wrote:

*Dear John* (I get lots of "Dear John" letters)*:*

*Your speech at our school really hit home. When I was little, my real dad left my mom and me. So, I don't remember him except for pictures and stuff. The one thing I do remember is the time he said he wanted me for the weekend and promised to take me to the zoo. My mom packed my suitcase, and I sat on the porch and waited for him from 8 a.m. to 6 p.m. Then, my mom made me come in. I hate that man, but inside I really love him. I never talk about him to my mom, because my adopted father is around.*

*John, it must be hard to lose your father in death.* (My dad died when I was 15.) *But it is harder knowing my dad is alive and doesn't want me. Thanks for listening.      Jason*

Just like everyone else, Jason desires to be wanted. He longs to be needed, and he prays to be loved. We all share similar desires, and when they're not met at home, we look elsewhere. Some look to friends. Some look to sports or music. Some look to relationships. Tragically, some may look to cigarettes, alcohol and other drugs or give themselves away sexually. Are you looking in healthy places to fill your emotional needs? I hope so.

## Self-esteem

When I was in elementary school I had a nickname. It was "Skinhead." My dad believed in the home haircut and owned Sears Craftsman clippers – gas powered, pull start, industrial strength. He could trim the grass around the house with those clippers.

He would say, "Son, come here." I would run out of the house. Dad would call me back in and set a stool in the center of the kitchen floor. "Sit down on the stool, son," he'd instruct. So, I'd sit down. Then he'd say, "Son, how much do you want off?" *Like it mattered.* Every time he buzzed my hair off everyone could see my scalp through my crewcut. So, friends called me Skinhead in elementary school, and it really hurt my feelings.

To treat yourself and others with more respect, ask yourself these three questions before you do or say something:
   **Is it nice?**
   • Is it loving toward that person?

- Will it hurt that person in any way?
- How would you feel if someone said or did that to you?

**Is it true?**

- Is it honorable to do or say?
- Where did you learn the information?
- If you hear a rumor, to whom should you go to clarify the information?

**Is it necessary?**

- Is it respectful towards yourself and others?
- How will your life be changed if you do or say it?
- How will someone else's life be changed if you do or say it?

With every decision, if you answer *yes* to these questions, you're on the right track. If you answer *no* to any of them, stop...and rethink your choice before you act.

In spite of the Skinhead nickname, I made it to seventh grade. I thought, "Great! New friends, new school, new teachers...*new nickname.*" I couldn't wait to hear my new nickname. When I did, however, I wished I had my old nickname back because the new nickname was... "Duckbutt." How embarrassing! Why *this* name? Well, I was shaped like an inflatable punching bag. My feet were big. My legs were short. My hips were wide. My shoulders were narrow. When I walked down the hallway, I looked like tennis shoes, knees and a baseball cap coming at you. They'd say, "Is John here yet? No. Wait...I see his feet; he'll be here any second now."

So picture the fuzz top, the body shape *and* black plastic-rimmed glasses...with little diamonds on the corners. They don't make them anymore because they destroyed kids' lives emotionally. It gets worse! Besides all of this, I had a swayback. My back was really arched. My butt stuck out so far they could have put backup lights on it. I would waddle when I walked, and that's why my friends called me Duckbutt. Whew! Though I kept it to myself, this hurt my feelings, too.

Still, at the end of the day I'd come home and look in the mirror. Who did I see? Duckbutt!!! All I could see was what was on the outside. I couldn't see what was on the inside. Yet it's what's on the inside that counts. Obviously, we're all different on the outside. We're boys and girls. We're black and white. We're tall and short. We're big and small. But what makes us special isn't what's on the outside. It's who we are on the inside. Think about your friends. You may be initially attracted to what's on the outside, but you love and make true friends with who they are on the inside. Always remember, it's what's on the inside that's most important for them as well as for you.

Think and plan ahead. What do you want to be remembered for after high school? Take this character test to find out:

| **Outside** | | **Inside** |
|---|---|---|
| your car | or | your character |
| your clothes | or | your convictions |
| your vanity | or | your values |

your peer group    or    your personality

your wealth    or    your worth

It's not **what** you are, it's **who** you are that counts.

Before others can fully know and accept you the way you are, you need to genuinely accept yourself first. Remind yourself of your value by counting and appreciating your blessings and successes. Completing the following action point will help. Expand your lists beyond ten if you can.

## *Action point: Feeling good about me*

Ten of my blessings are: (Blessings are the special gifts that are a part of you and your life.)

1. _____    6. _____

2. _____    7. _____

3. _____    8. _____

4. _____    9. _____

5. _____    10. _____

Ten of my successes are: (Successes are the things you've accomplished or earned.)

1. _____    6. _____

2. _____    7. _____

3. _____    8. _____

4. _____    9. _____

5. _____    10. _____

## Peer Pressure

In high school, I joined the swim team. One day, the cheer-leaders told us about an upcoming pep assembly. They stood in front of us and said, "You guys swim, right?"

We shot back, "Yeah, we swim."

They said, "Goldfish swim too, don't they?"

We replied, "Yeah, goldfish swim. What's the connection?"

They exclaimed, "Wouldn't it be great..."

Exasperated, we sighed, "Wouldn't what be great? You want us to race a goldfish in the pep assembly?"

They declared, "Do we have to explain everything to you? We think it would be great if you guys would swallow goldfish at the assembly...in front of the entire school!"

Until that moment, I'd never had the urge to swallow a goldfish. I never really wanted to swallow a goldfish. Nobody ever warned me not to, though. My mom never said, "Son, if you're at the park and somebody gets out a bag and inside the bag is water and a goldfish...say 'no'!"

So, I looked at the people volunteering. Many of these guys swam varsity and were incredibly popular. They were also in the party group and drank and did other drugs. As a non-user, I was excluded from parties and felt unaccepted. That explains why, when 10 guys volunteered to swallow the goldfish, I caved in (thinking this wouldn't hurt me) and reluctantly joined them.

That Friday, 1000 students filed into the auditorium for the pep assembly. Eleven goldfish circled in a ten-gallon aquarium set on a small table in the center of the stage. The swim team lined up and I, not wanting to do this, stood last in line. One by one the guys swallowed their goldfish. Eleven, ten, nine, eight, seven, six, five, four, three, two and then only one remained. That was one frightened goldfish, because all his buddies had disappeared!

The whole school, including all my friends, watched me as I wondered if I could catch the goldfish. I didn't have a net, so I used my chubby little fingers. Who was making me do this? *Nobody!* I was pressuring myself! This relates to all of life's questions. Have you figured out what you stand for, believe in and value?

Unfortunately, I fell for the *illusion* of peer pressure that day. Trembling I reached in, caught the last, lone goldfish, and held it in my hand. For a second I thought, what would happen if I just put it back? What if I just walked off stage? What's the worst thing that could occur? My mind fast forwarded to my five-year reunion. "There's the guy that didn't eat the goldfish..." Then, I envisioned my twenty-year reunion. "Hey, there's the fat bald guy that didn't swallow the goldfish...." At the time, I felt I *had* to do it. Did I? Who was making me? *I was!* Finally, I put the goldfish in my mouth and counted, "One, two (it was flipping), three." Gulp!!! I swallowed that poor-little-innocent fish because I was insecure and wanted to fit in with the group.

Peer pressure isn't always the pressure other people put on you. Peer pressure is often the pressure you put on yourself to be accepted by other people. To the degree that you need somebody else's *acceptance* or *approval* and fear their *rejection*, is the degree that you will feel pressure. It has less to do with the group, and more to do with you. For instance, when you look in the mirror and consider what you're going to wear or how you're going to style your hair, is it what you like the most...or what you feel your friends will like the most? Do you wonder what your friends will say about your attitudes, behaviors and choices as well? Think about it. I don't see me the way I actually see me, and I don't see me the way you actually see me. *I tend to see me the way I think, feel and perceive you see me.* So, peer pressure can be both *internal* as well as *external*, and both *positive* or *negative:*

<u>Positive Pressures</u>: (When conforming to these pressures, you *better* yourself.)

> The encouragement you receive to go out for a school play, run for a class office, try out for the team, get better grades, stop drinking or taking drugs, develop better study habits, develop self-confidence...

<u>Negative Pressures</u>: (When conforming to these pressures, you *hurt* yourself.)

> The pressure you feel to wear specific clothes, style your hair a certain way, spend time with the "in" group, put down or laugh at others, avoid talking with your parents, withhold affection from your family, drop out of class discussions or refrain from asking questions in class...

Too often we look through our friends' or the world's eyes to determine what we are going to believe or do. Like my dad used to say, "Son, if you don't stand for something... you'll fall for anything." **Remember, friends can't pressure you and make you do anything that you don't want to do.** You get to make the ultimate choice.

### *Action point: Recognizing peer pressure*
(Adapted from <u>Tough Turf</u> by: Bill Sanders)

**Four kinds of peer pressure.** (Write down examples of these in your life and whether they are internal or external pressures. Remember, you get to control your responses to both.)

- **"Follow the crowd"** peer pressure makes us want to be like everyone else.

- **"Can't be me"** peer pressure affects us when we constantly dream of being someone else.

- **"Afraid to try"** peer pressure keeps us from ever knowing our true potential. (People might laugh or I might fail...)

- **"Me pressuring me"** peer pressure applies to ourselves through our own self talk. (We hear ourselves thinking, "I can't do it. I'm not talented enough, good looking enough...)

## The Answer

When you're sitting in class and you don't know the answer, where do you tend to look? Down. The most exciting thing in life becomes the top of the desk. "I'm really busy right now," you may tell yourself. "I've got this great doodle going here. Don't interrupt me, because I don't know the answer."

But when you know the answer, where do you tend to look? Up! You may even raise your hand! You see, when you know the answer, you feel confident. When you have standards that cover all areas of your life, peer pressure miraculously goes away.

### *Action point: Memorizing ways to say "no"*

When somebody offers you cigarettes, alcohol or other drugs, have you figured out your answer ahead of time? Here's a list of ways to say "no." Try to memorize this and say it with one breath. *No, no thanks, not a chance, nope, no way, not for me, forget it, I'll think I'll pass, I never do the stuff, I don't believe in it, absolutely not, I'm not into destroying my brain cells, my buddy did it and he's dead, the answer is no, and don't ask again, and no thank you, I appreciate your kindness, but I simply will not be talked into changing my mind.*

Here's the secret. There is nothing physical in this world that can fill an emotional or spiritual hunger. Once you believe in your specialness, understand the sources of peer pressure and know the answers for you, life's pressures will subside and you'll gain a sense of control. It's who you are on the inside that counts, and your character will shine through your choices. So take responsibility. What choices will you make for you? Will you make them ahead of time, so you'll know what to do? Stand for something...or you may fall for anything.

# I Wanna Be a Muppet

by

M. K. DURAND FARLEY

# I Wanna Be a Muppet

by

## M. K. DURAND FARLEY

OK, first of all, I know that sounds strange but I am a HUGE Muppet fan. Occasionally, I even manage to catch an episode of *Sesame Street*, or S-Street as it commonly called by the super cool. At this very moment I'm listening to my CD called *Sesame Street Best* which contains some of my favorite songs like "C is for Cookie" and "Stand by Your Can" as performed by Oscar the Grouch.

It's odd but I feel like I have a connection with the Muppets. Maybe it's because in the year I was born, Sesame Street became the hottest new address on PBS. Or maybe it's *The Muppet Show* started right around the time I started performing on-stage. Perhaps it was all the excellent Muppet music or just the good ole fashioned Muppet mayhem. Nah, I prefer to think I was struck by Muppet magic.

Part of Muppet magic is that there is always something to be learned. The Muppets entertain, educate and uplift. It's not always right in your face but it's always there. So in grand Muppet-magic tradition, I'll warn you that there are life lessons hidden throughout this chapter. Don't worry though, I don't believe you'll have any trouble spotting them.

## And Jim Said "Let There Be Fur And Felt" And So It Was....

Did you know that **in all of creation there is no one exactly like you?** Not even if you have an identical twin. Which makes me think it would be more appropriate to call identical twins "people who look really really really really similar" instead. Out of the 50 billion or so people on this planet (we're still checking with Timbuktu), there are no two people with the same fingerprints, according to years of scientific data. That means that a great deal of extra time and effort was taken to make sure that you were an original, a one and only. Muppet magic embraces this principle from the get-go.

Before James Maury Henson (a.k.a. Jim Henson) came along, the word *"Muppet"* did not even exist. Henson made it up after creating his special combination of a marionette and a puppet. *He looked upon his creation and said "their name shall be called Muppets" and it was good.* *kermit 9:0210* Jim took great pride in his Muppet children. He ensured that each of his little Muppet weirdoes and frogs and bears (*Oh My!!*) were individually wrapped for freshness (oops, lost my train of thought)…were individual and unique creations. If you look you'll see that each Muppet was given many individual talents, an individual personality, and an individual purpose.

Let's talk about purpose for a minute because every man, woman and Muppet has one. **We weren't put here to simply get *THROUGH* it. We were put here to get *TO* it!** At the age of 17, I stopped believing in coincidences because too many weird things made too much sense when I put them together. So now I believe that there is a destination set for me. (Hmmm – is that what they mean by destiny? *The light bulb finally goes on*)

A poem by Frank Outlaw called *The 5 Watches*, talks about how your thoughts turn into your words, then into your actions, then into your character and so forth. But somewhere near the end he writes, "**Watch your character** for it becomes your destiny." Now "character" is essentially your personality. It's the collection of qualities that make you...you! I know you're thinking, "Well duh, who else would it make me?" but stay with me. We have all been assigned a purpose. We are also granted certain talents and specific personalities to help us achieve that purpose. Part of my purpose is to change pathetic attitudes about drug use and violence. I utilize my talents as a songwriter, vocalist and speaker along with the compassion, the concern and the sense of humor I have to achieve my purpose. Sounds easy enough, but there are some pitfalls that I've had to learn to avoid like not concerning myself with other people's opinions.

As humans, we worry that people won't like our personalities so we feel the need to change them. We worry that our talents won't be appreciated so we don't share them. This reaction is quite understandable in light of all the messages we're sent regarding looks, what's hot, what's not and who you should be. Think about all the ads featuring models with perfect hair, perfect skin and designer clothes. The ones who are so thin you're sure the word "sandwich" was removed from their vocabulary long ago. They tell us we use the wrong shampoo, wear the wrong clothes, we're not nearly cool enough and we eat too much. Then they reveal miracle products that will transform us into something better.

I'd like to save you a few wasted years by sharing a truth that I discovered awhile ago. **Identity** *(who you are)* **is far more important than image** *(who people think you are)*. You were born of Heaven and Earth and all that lie between...already great enough. (Oh by the way, that was one of those Muppet-magic subliminal life lessons just in case you missed it.)

## What Would A Muppet Do??

Of course, the normal response for us mere mortals is to alter our appearances and personalities to please those we want to impress. Because we all want friends. Homies and Homettes to hang with. Compadres to crack jokes with. Girlfriends to giggle with. Buddies to buy you ice cream and save you from eating today's mystery luncheon loaf in the cafeteria. No doubt about it, friends are important.

Bert and Ernie showed us that. They've remained friends for almost 30 years because of their similarities *(see striped shirts and Don King toupees)* and because they **accept and appreciate each others differences**. We, on the other hand, have to endure the lame excuses people use to exclude those who are not *"just like"* them. Not Bert and Ernie. Their skin color (OK, cloth color) is different, their head shapes are different, and some of their opinions are different. They've had a few disputes along the way, but nothing a spontaneous musical number couldn't fix. Ernie loves a good practical joke but he would never put Bert in danger or vice versa (which is Latin for "the other way around") because they know **friends should not be the cause of pain. They should be the relief from it.**

But they aren't the only Muppets with a life lesson. Take Ms. Piggy for instance. She has an attitude that I have always admired. Her attitude says, "Baby, I am a star! And if you don't know it, that's your problem not mine." Never in my life have I seen a more confident and determined pork product. When watching an episode of the *Muppet Babies*, it's plain to see that Piggy always intended to be a star and would never settle for less. She practiced and performed whenever she had the chance. She didn't allow the fact that she was supposed to be a salty, yet tasty, breakfast entree keep her from her dreams. She remained confident and managed to **turn stumbling blocks into stepping stones.**

Scientists discovered what's called the "Containment Theory" which I'll explain by way of an experiment (just call me Bill Nye, the Science Guy). First, get two identical 16-ounce bottles of soda. Remove the lid from one of them. What happened? Nothing. The liquid is perfectly content to stay inside the bottle and you can enjoy a refreshing beverage at your leisure.

Now, take the other 16-ounce bottle of soda, be sure your shoes are tied, shake it up a few times, hand it to someone who's gotten on your nerves, and politely ask them to open it for you. OK, what happened that time? I mean after the laughter, the gasping, the near drowning and your invigorating two mile sprint.

In my experiment, the 16-ounces of liquid no longer fit in the bottle it once called home. It overflowed its boundaries. That's what the "Containment Theory" is all about. Going beyond barriers that you didn't set and breaking the limits that have been imposed on you. There are people who were told they would never walk but go on to win marathons. Casey Pierretti roller-bladed across the United States of America after losing one of his legs to a drunk driver. Folks in wheel chairs are parachuting from planes. **Nothing is impossible because you are a living possibility**. Dr. Martin Luther King said that we are all destined for greatness. But like that soda in the bottle, sometimes, we need a little shakin' up to realize our potential.

If you don't believe that the impossible can be done, just check with Gonzo, the resident weirdo of the Muppet family. The first thing I like about Gonzo is that he is very odd and he doesn't care. My motto is: *I don't strive to be normal, I'm better than that*. I take pride in my individuality. After all, I am a unique creation. As are you. Another thing I like about Gonzo is his willingness to take risks. Now I would never shoot myself out of a cannon like he does, but unlike me he is already a Muppet and can do that without much physical pain. But **risks and challenges are good.** They guide you to your destiny.

Years ago, I started writing poetry, then song lyrics, then music for the song lyrics. Then I was asked to write plays, then speeches, then the opening and closing session for the Tennessee Governor's Conference. Then I was asked to write a chapter for this book. Each of these events was a new risk and a challenge for me. And my response was always the same. "I've never done that before," followed by "Oh what the heck! I'll give it a shot," followed by "WOW, I did that?" Every time Gonzo aims his cannon, he aims a little bit higher than the time before. The Reverend Jesse Jackson said "It is not your *aptitude* but your *attitude* that will determine your altitude."

That being the case, the Muppets must be way up there. I believe they display all of the attitudes essential for success in life. Oscar somehow manages to be polite even through his terminal grouchiness. Big Bird is always willing to help. Fozzy Bear never loses his sense of humor even though he always gets heckled. Beaker never deserts Dr. Bunsen Honeydew even after the experiments don't quite go as planned.

And then there's Kermit, my personal favorite (shhhh-don't tell the others), whose only goal on *The Muppet Show* and in every Muppet movie, is to uplift his friends and help them succeed. He never demanded to be the leader of the Muppets, but he rises to the challenge. He taught me that **we must do what we can, when we can, for whom we can.** Kermit The Frog sits on a ledge outside my bedroom door to remind me of that.

## Of Course We're Headed To Sesame Street!!

I want to be "on my way to where the air is clear." Where purple people with green noses, blue cows with orange hair, giant yellow birds that don't fly and a vast array of unknown species spanning a multitude of colors all get along. Where there's no crime and no drugs but instead, there is unity and harmony (sometimes in four parts). Where neighbors look out for each other, help one another and laugh together. Where seldom is heard a discouraging word and the skies are not cloudy all day. (Hey, that would make a great a song.)

I am a bleeding-heart idealist. (And no, that does not mean I need surgery) It means that I believe in the "they-all-lived-happily-ever-after" ending. I know it's possible because I believe in the human spirit, which is our determination to live and to achieve. You'll read, write and research a lot of history before you graduate from high school. As you pull all-nighters pondering which questions will be on the exam, notice that every time an attempt is made to squash the human spirit, it fights back and wins. It has survived every tragedy from the Holocaust to the Oklahoma City bombing. It has been to every protest and rally from the Civil Rights Movement to the March of Dimes Walk-A-Thon. That spirit is a gift that is given to each of us with the first breath we take. It's always there. Ready to stand for what is right and good and to turn its back on what is not. It <u>cannot</u> be crushed without your permission. **We are engineered for success and survival.**

## I Am Muppet…Hear Me Roar!!

Jim Henson started out with just a couple of Muppets and ended up with an entire corporation. He created shows that are translated into dozens of languages and seen in more than 100 countries around the world. A grin somehow finds its way to my face at the mention of Muppets. To this day I still hear The Count saying "One…ah ah ah ah, two…ah ah ah ah ah…." I see Grover spastically running back and forth to show me *"near and far."*

Henry David Thoreau wrote, **"Be not simply good, be good for something."** When Jim Henson passed away in 1990…I noticed. Jim was remembered for his contributions to learning, the enormous and continued success of the Muppets, his kind spirit and gentle caring nature.

Ninety years from now, what is it that you want people to remember about you? It doesn't necessarily have to be that you were a multi-millionaire, an NBA star, or that you won the most Grammies or Oscars. Those things are nice but remember that **profit is not always measured in money and character is not always measured by status**. You could hope to be remembered for your compassion, your commitment to excellence, your generosity, your accomplishments, or for being a phenomenal parent someday. Whatever it is, write it down and keep it close. Every so often, check to see how close you are to accomplishing the things on your list.

Personally...I would like to be remembered as the guy who spent his life spreading the Muppet magic and building Sesame Streets around the world. If all goes according to plan, the next time someone asks, "Can you tell me how to get, how to get to Sesame Street?" you'll be able to say, "Why yes...these are Bugle Boy jeans I'm wearing." (just kidding) I hope you'll be able to say, "Why yes, that's where I **live...happily ever after**."

# Life is a Roller Coaster…

## *Enjoy the Ride!*

by

Jennifer Esperante Gunter

**Pre TEEN POWER**

# Life is a Roller Coaster...
## *Enjoy the Ride!*

by

JENNIFER ESPERANTE GUNTER

### "If you're happy and you know it, clap your hands! (*clap, clap*)

If you're happy and you know it,
clap your hands! (*clap, clap*)
If you're happy and you know it,
and you really want to show it,
if you're happy and you know it,
clap your hands! (*clap, clap*)"

Remember that silly song we used to sing when we were little? Well, we're older now, so here's my question. What do you do if you're not? You know...not happy? What do you do if you're flat-out-honest-to-goodness MAD, UPSET, HURT, or FRUSTRATED...what do you do? Yell at someone you love? Make someone else mad so you'll feel better? Or even worse...put your fist through a door? Bang your head on a wall? Well, that's how some people handle their emotions... Yes, that's how I used to handle my own.

A few years ago, whenever I got angry or frustrated, I would run to the nearest bathroom. That was my escape from the world. I would close the door (okay, okay – actually I would slam it shut), lock it, and then I would cry – sometimes for a long, long time. And if I was really feeling hopeless, I would resort to hurting myself. I would bang MY head on a wall. I guess I was trying to stop the hurt *inside* by making myself hurt *outside*.

What's funny about growing up is that we are taught our ABC's and 1,2,3's...we're taught "Please" and "Thank-you"...and the difference between "Left" and "Right." We learn important information we need for the thing called "LIFE." By the time we are five we can make our own beds, tie our own shoes, and maybe even make our own lunches! But we can get to be fifty years old without ever learning what to do with painful emotions. We have never learned how to enjoy the ride on "The Roller Coaster of Life"!

––––––––––

Remember that awesome roller coaster at your favorite amusement park?

When the roller coaster climbs up, you and your buddies (or buddy-ettes, if you're a girl) get all excited. Maybe you're the type like me that holds on tight 'cuz deep inside you're super-duper scared the bar might unlatch, and you'd fall out and go SPLAT! Or maybe you're like my sisters – the type that puts your hands up in the air when you get to the "Point of No Return."

You're ready for the thrilling moment of near-death experience…and you LOVE IT! It's MASSIVE CHAOS! People are screaming like crazy. Hair is flying everywhere! If you could only capture a Kodak moment of those faces – mouths wide open, ears sticking out like Dumbo, nostrils flaring so wide open bugs could fly in! And, no matter what "type" of roller coaster rider you are, the bottom line is: "When you hop on – you have to experience the WHOLE RIDE…the UP and the DOWN!" So, let's put it this way. LIFE IS LIKE A ROLLER COASTER.

Your UP moments are when you are EXCITED, HAPPY and ENJOYING experiences that you wish you could repeat. The DOWN times are when life is SCARY, CONFUSING, and UNCOMFORTABLE – the times you wish you could erase. But, just like the roller coaster goes up and down…so does life. It can't all be happy – **after all, how would you know what it was to be happy if you had never been sad?**

So, when you're in the DOWN times: *What do you do?* Do you stay calm, knowing the ride will eventually go back up again? Or do you go crazy like the people on the roller coaster? You worry, complain and feel miserable, thinking it will stay that way  forever?…or do you need help learning *how to enjoy the ride?*

I speak all over the country and have been blessed to work with teens from Hawaii to New York and as far away as Canada and Guam. I help teens "survive" the DOWN times when they think they can't. When I share my personal stories of struggle and success, people often write to me afterwards, seeking help and guidance. Just yesterday, I opened a letter from a student, and I couldn't help but almost cry. A young girl told me that she couldn't even look in the mirror because she felt so bad about herself. She said she hated herself...and that she had tried to commit suicide and wanted to try again.

I felt helpless. Without her phone number, I could only write back and hope it wouldn't be too late. I didn't know what had happened in her life, but I could feel her pain and loneliness, and realized that she was trying to get rid of it by getting rid of herself. I wanted to look her in the eyes and say, "Nothing in life...NOTHING! is so bad that you can't get help, and win the battle in the end. NOTHING is worth taking your own life away! Hang on...hang on!" It was obvious. She was trying to eliminate her DOWN time by eliminating herself.

Sometimes the DOWN time is the death of someone you love. Maybe one of you reading this book lost one of your parents when you were little...and that was really hard. Maybe you've never dealt with that loss and have been pretending for years that you are over it...but deep inside, you are really angry and confused. I'll bet that some of you constantly fight with your parents. You don't seem to understand each other. It's frustrating and it hurts! You wish you could run away from the pain and hide.

Others of you live in a world of "masks." When you go to school you *pretend* everything is fine. Maybe you're even popular and *act* happy, but deep inside you're having a really hard time. You handle your pain by keeping it hidden...desperately hoping that one day it will all go away. Some escape these feelings by smothering their emotions with drugs or alcohol. AHHHH! It makes them feel so good...for a while anyway.

Our roller coasters have all gone DOWN at one point in time...in other words, we've all had pain and challenges. The question is – what do you do about it? I learned what to do with mine when I heard a speaker who's message changed my life. He had been badly burned and paralyzed from the waist down, forever. Listening to him, I could barely imagine what my life would be like without being able to walk, run, swim, or have the freedom to do ANY-THING I wanted, WHENEVER I wanted, WITHOUT having to think. Then, he said it – the words that made the difference. He said: **"Remember – IT'S NOT WHAT HAPPENS TO YOU – IT'S WHAT YOU DO ABOUT IT."** And those few words, changed my life.

I realized that I COULDN'T BE A VICTIM OF WHAT HAPPENED TO ME! I couldn't sit there making the same ol' excuses anymore:

"Well, in my family we don't say 'I love you.' That's just the way we are."

"I'll never be able to be as 'successful' as them. I just don't have it in me."

"It's all my parents' fault!"

"I got hurt before – so I'm too scared to try again."

"Life just isn't fair."

I couldn't use any of those excuses. I couldn't use an excuse, period. I couldn't even blame it on my imaginary friend! The speaker was forcing me to take responsibility for MY LIFE. Again, **"IT'S NOT WHAT HAPPENS TO YOU – IT'S WHAT YOU DO ABOUT IT. IT'S NOT WHAT HAPPENS TO YOU, IT'S HOW YOU REACT, HOW YOU THINK, HOW YOU HANDLE IT!"** And I realized that I had to create my own destiny… 'cuz if I didn't, something or someone else would!

---

## I learned an important lesson about how to create my own destiny one night…

when my sister said she loved me. You see, in my family, I was "The Princess." **I had my own room.** It was white with pink frills. I had Barbies galore – the Barbie dream house, the Barbie pool, and even the awesome Ken. I had all the Hello Kitty collections, along with little purses and dresses, and even hats. And, my room was spotless – everything in perfect order. Yes, **I had my own room**, and I was only eight.

My sisters Mary Jean (we called her Jin Jin) and Irene were ten and twelve. **They shared a room.** It doesn't make much sense, does it? That I was the youngest and I had my own room. Wasn't Irene supposed to have her own room? After all, she WAS the oldest! Either way, I was happy…but never really knew how Jin Jin and Irene really felt…until that night!

A couple of years ago, my sister Jin Jin came to visit, and told my mom and I that she was having a hard time in her marriage. She had to make a tough decision – to leave her husband or stay. I hadn't seen or spoken with my sister in a really long time. Though we kind of grew apart, I wanted desperately to help her now…but to be honest, I was scared to butt in. I was *The Baby* in the family – who was I to offer advice to an older sister who was married and had two beautiful children?

Ever have a hard time talking with your family? Well, it was happening here. Sitting and talking in my mom's living room, the three of us weren't getting anywhere – a mom and two daughters trying desperately to communicate and getting nowhere. A FAMILY WANTING SO MUCH TO HELP AND GET HELP BUT FEELING TOO SCARED AND EMOTIONALLY UNEDU-

CATED TO KNOW HOW. It was definitely a DOWN time on our roller coaster. As we struggled through the night trying so hard to talk to each other, my mom walked out and left my sister and I alone…and it was then the truth came out.

Nothing I said seemed to break the ice. I offered her my love…and she rejected it. "There is nothing you can do," she said. "You have changed so much anyway." I agreed. I had changed…for the better. I had finished four years of college, had majored in the life-changing study of Psychology, and had two years of personal counseling. All this had helped me mature mentally and emotionally far more than I could have EVER imagined. But, Jin Jin just kept saying, "You wouldn't understand."

Her rejection hurt so much…that I finally blurted out, "You think you have it really hard and I have everything so easy – so there's no way I could understand the least bit of what you're going through. You think my life is perfect and I have everything!" I rambled on as tears ran down my face. I lost it and cried like a baby! I felt like running to the bathroom – my old escape.

Jin Jin said, "That's right – there is no way you could ever understand. You have everything you want – a big house, a happy marriage, no problems…You have everything! You always did." She continued telling me all the reasons why I wouldn't understand, until she finally said, "…and when we were kids, YOU HAD YOUR OWN ROOM!"

When she said those words, years of trapped pain and misery were finally released. She burst out in tears, and I cried even more, sorry she felt that way without ever knowing her true feelings. I sobbed, "You know sometimes I wish I was ugly, that I didn't have my house, and that my marriage was terrible, that I just didn't have it together – because maybe, just maybe, if I was all messed up – you would like me better…and you would believe I could help!"

There we sat – my sister 26 – and me 24 – crying like babies because of something that happened when we were 8 and 10 years old. For years, we both felt that "life wasn't fair" – Jin Jin because I had my own room, and me because I thought she didn't like me. We had been dealing with our pain for all those years…IN SILENCE, pretending that nothing hurt when it really, really did.

What did we learn that night? First off, that silence doesn't work. Secondly, Jin Jin discovered that my life wasn't so perfect after all. I shared with her the struggles I had experienced that she never knew about. She found out that I cared for her…and I realized that she cared for me far more than I ever knew. The big risk we took to say what we truly felt brought us: FREEDOM! Freedom from having our love smothered under a layer of fear, frustration, and jealousy. And I learned that instead of banging your head on a wall, putting your fist through a door, or even resorting to drugs and alcohol to escape from your pain – the best way of dealing with problems is to COMMUNICATE, BE HONEST, and ASK FOR HELP!

That conversation marked an eventful day for my sister and I. We had turned a terrible DOWN time into an UP time! My sister hugged me and I could feel her love oozing all over! It was INCREDIBLE! We ended that night with the words my family is not used to saying – "I love you" – and I can tell you it felt sooooo good. No longer did I want to use the excuse, "My family doesn't say that," because just like that speaker said – we create our own destinies! And, that night…I was *re-creating* my own!

So, do yourself a favor. Don't handle your painful situation by pretending it's not there. Don't hold it inside where it will keep on hurting you, and force you to hate yourself (like the student), bang your head on a wall (like me) or turn to substance abuse like thousands of unlucky teenagers across America. **Remember that if you reach out, there are people that will help you.** If you muster up the courage to ask for HELP, there will be people who will say, "I am here." It may be *your* sister, your brother, mom, dad – or maybe even a speaker like me. But no matter what, there is always someone that will care.

I hope you have been inspired by reading my chapter to discover positive and healthy ways to work through your pain. Just remember that life doesn't have to be so miserable, nor lonely. Painful events from the past don't have to live on in the form of anger or jealousy forever. With love, honesty and communication – you really can

LET GO...THROW YOUR HANDS UP...
and ENJOY THE RIDE...

ON THE ROLLER COASTER OF LIFE!

GO FOR IT! AND HAVE A GREAT TIME!

# It Takes GUTS to Make a Difference

by
NORM HULL

# It Takes GUTS
# to Make a Difference

by
NORM HULL

You never know when the opportunity will arise to make a difference in this world. There won't be any warning sirens or large posters, and no one will whisper in your ear telling you that your chance is at hand.

However, through the years, people have told me, *"You have so much potential."* I've always asked myself, *"The potential for what?"* Unfortunately, no one ever answers that question; they never fill in the blank. People merely say we have "the potential to become a doctor," "the potential to become an influential leader," or "the potential to become someone's very best friend." This used to frustrate me until I realized that it was up to ME to fill in the blank!

It's all a matter of choice. Choosing to do nothing is in itself a choice. However, it's as easy to do something as it is to do nothing. Because we have the ability to choose our own paths, we need to seize the opportunities before us! I use the acronym GUTS to demonstrate how you can make your dreams come true. You have the power!

# G - Goals

Personally, I have found that once I set a goal for myself, I can decide when, where, and how to use my own potential in achieving it. But success comes from achieving our own goals, not the goals of others. Have you ever worked hard towards a goal, achieved it, and felt disappointed in the end? Perhaps this happened because the goal wasn't really your own. You and I have such a strong desire to please and impress other people that we often lose track of our own dreams and ambitions. We need to look deep down inside ourselves to determine what we truly want.

I've visited schools and observed student leaders planning exciting projects and activities, only to have the activity or project not work. The students always seem to wonder, "what went wrong?" In most cases, group goals are not achieved because the plan isn't solid or because different students have different ideas about what the end result (or goal) should be. Any goal, regardless if it is being set for a single person or for an entire group of people, must be written down. This way, those working toward the goal can have their sights clearly set on a desired result, and will always be reminded of what needs to be done to accomplish that goal.

# U - Understanding

A teacher friend of mine told me a story about one of her students that really touched my heart. Her student, James, lived in the city with his younger sister and older brother. He didn't see much of his father, and his mom worked several jobs just to feed and clothe her children. James' neighborhood is poor and run down, but the people are nice and respectful. James is a fairly good student, and he tries hard to be a good kid and set an example for others.

Recently, James behavior began to change for the worse. His teacher frequently noticed him sitting in the back of the room sleeping during class. Even though she'd wake him up and ask him to pay attention, James would soon fall asleep again. Frustrated, she sent James to the principal's office. But James wouldn't tell the principal why he couldn't stay awake, so he was given an on-campus suspension and had to help the custodians clean the campus.

One day my friend approached James while he was walking down the hall and asked if she could speak with him. She told James that she really liked him as a person, but that she couldn't accept his classroom naps.

Fighting back the tears, James finally began to explain. *"My brother sells drugs because our family needs the money for food and rent."* He continued, *"Some people who bought from him didn't like what they received, so they've been coming back at all hours in the night looking for him and taking gunshots at our apartment. They still haven't been caught. I stay up all night watching out the window, making sure that if they come back, I can warn my mom and take my sister to a safe part of the apartment. I am pretty tired when I get to school. I guess I feel safe in your class and it becomes easy to finally rest. I know that it bothers you so I try really hard to stay awake but I don't always make it. I am sorry I have caused you so many problems."*

At that moment, my friend felt horrible for James. She now understood the situation and took steps to help James and his family. Her feelings had changed from anger and disappointment to sadness and wanting to help.

Understanding was the key, which is vital in relationships of any kind. Without understanding, even the tightest bonds can be broken between friends and family. Relationships can be severely damaged. However, if you have **GUTS**, you will put your own feelings aside and try to understand what the other person is dealing with. Then it becomes easier to see solutions and help them through difficult times. This makes your relationship with that person even stronger.

## T - Trust

Growing up in a military family, we had the opportunity to travel throughout the world. When I was younger, my dad was stationed in Paris, France. Because I didn't speak the language, I had a hard time making friends. As a result, I really didn't enjoy or appreciate my time in France.

We lived in apartment complex which housed lots of families with young children. Although there were always many playmates nearby, my brothers and I were particularly excited when we discovered our mother's stomach growing larger and larger. A new addition to our family was on the way!

The day my youngest brother decided to enter the world, things became very hectic. As expected, our father had to take our mom to the hospital and trusted me with the responsibility of watching my two younger brothers, Derrick and Kevin. Before he left, Dad said to me fatherly, *"Stay inside, and I will be back shortly."* It seemed a simple request at the time. But as soon as they drove away, Derrick and Kevin ran to me and said *"Hey, let's go outside!"* I immediately replied, *"No, dad said we can't."* My brothers then started to whine and pressure me, saying things like, *"It's no fun when you're in charge! C'mon, we won't get caught! Dad won't find out. . . it's such a great day. . .let's go out and play!"*

Two against one is hard, especially when the "two" are your brothers. I admit, I also wanted to go outside. It didn't help that we heard all of our friends playing and calling to us to join them. Finally, I gave in. We were outdoors having a blast until suddenly, one of my brothers yelled out, "*There he is!*" All three of us looked and saw dad's car pulling into the garage. We quickly ran in through the back door, hopped on the sofa, and turned on the television. We were darn sure we had outsmarted dad.

When he entered the apartment, dad came directly over to me and asked if everything had been okay while he was out. I nodded yes. My brothers seemed impressed with the way I was handling matters. Dad then asked another question – the one I dreaded. *"Did you go outside?"* I immediately blurted out *"No!"* His eyes remained locked on me as he again asked, *"Did you go outside?"* I could have sworn that he had asked me the very same question just moments earlier. My brothers continued to stare at me, avoiding eye contact with our dad. He knew I was lying, but I just couldn't admit it. The room filled with tension. Finally, I broke the silence. *"Dad, I've let you down...."* I had indeed shattered his trust in me, and it took years to get it back.

We all have people in our lives who know how to get under our skin and encourage us to do things that are wrong or inappropriate. They challenge us with statements like, *"I dare you"* and call us names like *"wimp"* or *"chicken."* They may even threaten us with comments like, *"Everyone else does; what's wrong with you?"* Curiously, our closest friends know how to get us to react in a certain way because they know our most guarded secrets. Real friends, however, will never ask us to do things which might cause us grief or trouble.

Before you betray someone's trust or confidence in you, stop to consider the impact of your decision. One bad decision (like mine) won't wreck you, but I've learned the hard way that it's difficult to regain someone's trust once you've lost it. Take the time to think about the situations in your life where someone puts their faith and trust in you. Make sure you don't let those individuals down. It takes **GUTS**, but in the end you'll be glad that you did the right thing and kept the trust.

## S - Support

In seventh grade, I had a friend named Edgar. He was the popular type: taller than most of us, stronger than most of us, and better in sports than all of us. He had a ten-speed bike. Mine was a single-speed bike so it was very hard to keep up with him. But Edgar was a cool kid, so he always waited for me instead of leaving me in the dust.

Edgar matured faster that the average kid, meaning he had hair. Not just on his head, either. . . Edgar had hair on his chin! His beard hairs curled around creating a little patch in the center of his chin, so all the girls thought he was macho. A lot of kids became his friends just so they could be around someone who looked a little bit older.

It didn't take long for Edgar to discover that the other kids liked him for what he had instead of what he was. He didn't have many "real" friends, only pretenders. To others he looked popular but inside he felt used and very alone.

Have you ever noticed people who hang around others just to appear popular? People tend to cluster around those who have what they want and then ridicule others for being different. Edgar was different. The crowd just liked his differences. Why then, do some people get "picked on" because of their differences?

If you are looking for a reason to pick on someone, there are plenty to choose from. Most things are visible to the eye (e.g., size, weight, eye color, hair, skin type). But it's not what's on the outside that makes a person good or bad; it is what lies on the inside that counts.

To be successful in this world, you need to support others, regardless of their differences. It would be a boring world if everyone were exactly like you! So value the differences between yourself and others and appreciate people for who they are!

## Always remember, it takes GUTS!

Your **G**oals should be determined only by you. Others may offer input, suggestions, and even a little guidance, but the final decision needs to be made by you. Before you judge others, make an attempt to **U**nderstand their point of view. **T**rust is developed over years and can be destroyed in a moment, so think before you act. Finally, **S**upport your friends regardless of what they may look like on the outside.

Yes, it takes **GUTS** to make a difference in this world. However, I'm 100% sure that you have what it takes to reach the top and help others along the way! That, my friend, is a difference that will last forever.

# The Winning Difference!

by
DENNIS MITCHELL

# The Winning Difference!

by
### Dennis Mitchell

Has anybody ever told you that you have a bad attitude? Has anybody told you that you have a good attitude? If you are like most of us, the answer to both questions is the same: YES. But has anyone ever really told you what an attitude is? Probably not! All that you know for sure is that you have one, right?

Perhaps you have heard that "attitude is everything?" However, attitude without action is worthless. The Chinese have a saying, "those who sit, always on bottom!" Henry Ford said that "action is the real measure of intelligence!" I believe that a positive mental <u>attitude</u>, when it is combined with <u>action</u> is THE WINNING DIFFERENCE!

Action is easy to understand, but where do we get our attitude? Our attitude comes from our expectations. Expectations come from our beliefs. Our beliefs come from how we see ourselves and others. Simply put, our attitude is the way we look at the world around us.

# What Goes In, Comes Out!

In his classic book "As a Man Thinketh," James Allen says that our mind is like a rich fertile garden where either flowers or weeds will grow. Weeds grow naturally; they don't need fertilizer. Flowers need more care, but when they grow, they multiply and spread happiness and joy!

What are you planting into the rich, fertile garden of your mind? Are you planting seeds of positive, uplifting thoughts that will drive you forward? Or are you allowing weeds to grow by sprinkling trashy television programs, movies, and song lyrics into your head?

Unfortunately, many people don't feel good about themselves. Often times, this is a result of what others have said to them and about them. If you were constantly told that you were dumb, stupid, or ugly and you believed these statements to be true, you probably wouldn't feel too good about yourself. You might even tell yourself, "I'm just a loser!" However, if you were told that you were intelligent, good looking, and fun to be with, and you believed these statements, you'd probably like yourself.

It really matters what kind of thoughts are planted into your head. Those thoughts become the seeds from which either flowers or weeds will sprout. So just like we need to fertilize a garden, we also need to fertilize our minds with positive thoughts by reviewing positive books, tapes, and materials to keep our mental gardens fresh and alive.

# An Attitude Is Contagious!

To keep a positive attitude, we must associate with positive, uplifting people. But this can be difficult because there are far more negative people among us than there are positive soles. People who are negative believe that the only way to bring themselves up is to put others down. Obviously they fail to realize that when they are throwing dirt, they're constantly losing ground! But if you take good care of yourself, you can give a part of yourself away to help other people. And there is no greater joy than helping others live a better life.

I feel that I can talk about the importance of a good attitude because when I was growing up I had an attitude that was so bad, I could brighten up a whole room. . . just by leaving! I had "mental body odor." I was hanging with the wrong crowd, making the wrong choices, and my attitude led me to do things that took me in and out of juvenile detention centers.

When I finally turned my life around, I wanted to help others avoid the pitfalls I had fallen into. One thing I did was to co-write the song "Choices." It is a biography of my life, and It goes like this; *"Eight and a half in the state pen with an attitude to get out and start clockin', doing my time for my crime I owe this, my child was killed by a drunken motorist. Reality struck like a nine at point blank, I got my head together and I gotta think, I made a bad choice and I did my time, now I'm redesigning my future with my mouth and my mind. A choice can change your life, you can choose peace or you can choose strife, it really makes a difference what you choose to do, right or wrong it comes back to you. An educated mind is the key to what you need, a positive attitude will help you to succeed, like my homie Dennis who corrected his mistakes, the choice to do right is the difference that it makes. Don't fall into the traps of drugs and crime, choose your friends wisely or you will end up doing time. You can change your life or your life can change you, it all depends on what you choose to do!"*

Take it from someone who knows first hand that crime, drugs, gangs and violence are weeds which will spread and spoil the garden. Let the mistakes I made be an example for you of "what <u>not</u> to do." Also realize that, no matter how bad things get, you can change them for the better, if you are willing to make sacrifices and work very hard. However, if you make the right choices from the start, and keep a positive attitude, you'll be miles ahead in the long run.

## Get Out Of Your Own Way!

When it comes to being successful, many people get in their own way. Many people actually have a fear of success. They are afraid of what others might say, or worse, they are afraid of new experiences and opportunities. Every opportunity carries with it the chance to grow and prosper, but we might fall short of our expectations. However, by confronting our fears, we find the courage to overcome them!

The only way to truly fail is to give up. It is far better to try something and not get the result you want, than it is to do nothing and succeed at doing nothing! Never allow fear to come between you and your dream. Those who achieve greatness have faced their fears and moved beyond them. Successful people do not always succeed, but they never stop trying.

## What Do You See?

Why do some people see the glass of water as half empty while others see the same glass as half full? Negative people look at the glass and say it's half empty. Positive people look at the same glass and say it's half full. The only difference is negative people are taking water from the glass while positive people are adding water to the glass. It all depends on how you look at life. *Your perception is everything.* Negative people look for problems; positive people look for solutions. Negative people complain; positive people celebrate. Negative people look out the window and notice a smudge on the glass while positive people look out with a clear view and see a beautiful world.

As you read this book, you will get a lot of great advice to help you live a happier, better life throughout your teens. Those that use this wisdom will have an easier time in the years ahead. Those that think of this book as only "words on paper" will probably apply nothing, and as a result, will have a more challenging time. After all, good information is useful only when it is used.

## Who's In Charge?

I believe that the most devastating thing that can happen to anyone is to have their children murdered. My son was taken from me by a drunk driver when he was only five years old. Because I was so busy being part of the me generation (causing problems instead of creating solutions), I was in prison at the time it happened. One of the things that hurts me the most is I didn't tell Little Dennis that I loved him before he died. Now I make certain that I tell all my loved ones how I feel about them. I urge you to do the same. Who knows what the future holds, and how long each of us will be around?

Just last week, I read a story in our local paper. Six teens from a nearby high school went to a graduation party to celebrate with their friends. On the way home, they flipped their car and it landed on the driver, killing him and sending three severely injured passengers to the hospital. They had all been drinking, and the result was death! Without alcohol, the outcome would have been different and their parents would have attended a graduation instead of a funeral. It was a senseless tragedy that could have been avoided.

I bet you know someone that has been involved in an alcohol related accident at your school or in your community. For every action in our lives, there is an opposite reaction. For every cause, there is an effect. We can learn from the mistakes of others.

## How Would You Respond?

One day, as I was driving on the freeway coming from Coeur d'Alene, Idaho to Spokane, Washington, I happened to look over at the truck next to me. For no apparent reason, the driver was waving his fist, yelling and cussing at me, then he flipped me off and I could see him mouthing the word "Nigger." Growing up, my mother taught me that a "Nigger" has no color or gender, but is actually a term for an ignorant person. Which one of us was being ignorant? Was I supposed to return his anger? I had a choice. Rather than joining him in his game, I smiled, and instead of giving him "the finger," I gave him two – the peace sign! He was stunned and had no idea how to deal with my act of kindness.

To react is negative, to respond is positive. I made a decision a long time ago not to allow other people to control my attitude. By having the right attitude, you too will rise to overcome adversity where you'll be in control of your life and your destiny!

## What Do You *Bee*lieve?

According to the law of aerodynamics the bumblebee can't fly. Its body is too heavy in proportion to its wings. (It's a good thing that a bumblebee does not smoke, drink and hang around with negative peers who are buzzing around telling each other what they cannot do.) The bumblebee does not know the law of aerodynamics, so it flies like crazy!!! Like the bumblebee, we, too, can do amazing things!

The bumblebee acts out of instinct, but you and I have the power of choice. We can choose to do great things, or we can let the negative beliefs of others weigh us down, causing us to do little or nothing with our lives. Our challenge is to become all we are capable of becoming. However, if we are going to BEE all we possibly can BEE, we need to do our best in school and choose positive friends.

## A Final Thought

Remember, you are the only one that can make it happen for you. Keep a positive healthy attitude, take action, and help others along the way. This is THE WINNING DIFFERENCE! Good Luck, and Godspeed!

# The Domino Theory

by
MIKE PATRICK

# The Domino Theory

by
### MIKE PATRICK

When I was sixteen my whole life changed in a single play on a football field. It was a chilly September evening. I was severely injured when my face mask caught on an All-state running back's knee pad. As I lay there on the wet grass, questions started racing through my mind. What is happening? Why is this happening? Why is this happening to me?

I had broken my neck and became paralyzed from the middle of my chest down. In the months in the hospital following my injury I went through all the stages of grief including anger, depression and denial. I was going to walk again. Two months after I got hurt, I remember my doctor was talking to me and my physical therapist was in the room. Dr. Church was having a hard time saying what he needed to say. I had questions for him, but I couldn't ask them. Only after he had left the room did I ask the physical therapist what I really wanted to know. "Was he trying to tell me I would never walk again?"

"Yes," she said. Her voice sounded tired. She looked down at the floor.

Asking questions is not always easy. At times they may seem nearly impossible to ask. At times you may not feel strong enough to hear the answer. But asking questions helps us to understand our lives. And like in a domino snake, one question can lead to another and another and finally clarity and understanding can help give us strength.

Months after my injury another doctor told me I would need to learn everything about my body and my care so I would be able to manage and direct those responsible for assisting me in my daily living needs. I wasn't ready to do that then. I was sixteen. I was denying the fact I would never walk again.

Now, twenty-six years later, I know the importance of asking questions. It's taken many lessons along the way. This past year I spent four-and-a-half months in the hospital. My heart stopped several times. They implanted a pacemaker. They removed a kidney. They fought a series of infections. And every time a nurse or a doctor came into my room I asked what was on my mind. "What medication is this? What is it for? Are there any side effects? How will I have to change my daily life to adjust to this?" You get the idea. I have learned there are no bad questions. I have learned I need to be specific in my question if I want a specific answer that is helpful.

I'm a professional speaker who travels the country doing programs for young people. I always leave time for questions and kids always have lots of them.

My all-time favorite question happened one day when a fourth grader asked me, "How do you get gas?"

"It usually comes from eating a school lunch." I said.

"No, no, that's not what I meant," he said. "What I mean is, how do you get gas in that special van you drive?"

"That's a different question. If you don't ask a specific question, you probably won't get a specific answer."

I want you to think about the questions you ask before you ask them, to make sure someone knows what it is you are talking about. I call my school program "Think About It." I believe if you think about a problem and what it is you need to know to help you, chances are pretty good you'll ask good questions and find the answer. So I tell kids, "The problem isn't the issue, the issue is how you deal with the problem."

Any problem can be a big problem if it's yours. Don't let anyone tell you that what is bothering you isn't important. If you think it is a big deal, then it is a big deal and you have to figure it out.

One day in a school that was built because a tornado had destroyed the previous school, a third grader asked, "What would you do if a tornado came by your house?" I told him I would go into my basement on the elevator I have in a closet. Once I got in the basement, I would go to the corner of the house facing the direction the tornado was coming from, and hope it didn't hit my house.

Kids often ask questions relating to their life experience. Those students were all very aware of tornadoes because the one that destroyed their old school had also destroyed many of their houses. The tornado had a tremendous impact on their lives. They had tornado drills in school and their parents had plans for them at home should another one come. The same kind of thing happens after a hurricane, flood, fire or any other disaster.

Kids need to be able to make sense of things by putting themselves in a particular position. I am a quadriplegic, which means I have lost the function or partial function of all four limbs. I use a power wheelchair to get around and I drive a specially-equipped van from my wheelchair using hand controls.

One day many years ago in a third grade class, a girl asked how you get hurt diving. We were talking about ways of damaging your spinal cord and becoming paralyzed. Kids came up with things like car and motorcycle accidents, diving, falling out of a tree, skiing and a few more. The reason she wanted to know was her sister was on the high school diving team and she wanted to make sure it didn't happen to her sister. I told her about diving into water that is too shallow and hitting your head on the bottom, or diving into dirty water and hitting something just under the surface. I always tell kids to know how deep the water is and go into dirty or cloudy water feet first.

Some young people need to know all the details. One fourth grader asked a series of questions all the way through my program. Every few minutes, he wanted to know another detail about the game. He asked what quarter it was, how much time was left, what color uniforms my team was wearing, how big the ball carrier was I was trying to tackle, was it a running play or a passing play, what was the score; it was amazing. I'll bet he asked a dozen questions.

I think he had an older brother or two playing football and he wanted to make sure they didn't get themselves in the exact situation I was in or they could get hurt too. He was probably thinking about himself too and wondering if he'd ever been in just that situation. Over the years kids have asked me all kinds of questions about the play, the game, that day, would I play football again if I could? Kids are very curious and curiosity is a key to learning.

One day in a school the week after Fire Prevention Week, a little guy raised his hand and wanted to know what I would do if there was a fire in my house. I told him I would go out the back door, down the ramp and away from my house. Then he said, "What if you couldn't get out the back door?"

"I'd go out the front door and sit on the front step and wait for the fire department to get there."

His hand shot up again and this time he asked, "What if you couldn't get out the front door?"

"I'd go in the shower and turn the shower on."

Boom! Up goes his hand again, and this time it was, "Would you take a cold shower?"

I told him I would after my hot water ran out! Guess what? His hand shot up again. "What if there was someone in the shower?"

I said, "I would tell them, hey, the house is burning down. We'd better get out!"

My little pal wasn't done. Up went his hand again and he asked, "What if it was a woman?"

Since I live alone, I told him that probably wasn't very likely to happen. It was absolutely amazing, he was doing exactly what I talk about in my program and asking specific questions. The progression of his line of questioning was very logical and very well thought out. He was thinking and that was very cool.

Some of the questions I get can be pretty funny. Others show some fairly disturbing things about what is going on in some kids minds. It worries me to see the degree of violence they find acceptable and even funny. I told you earlier I can't feel anything from the middle of my chest down. I tell that to every group and tell them if they scratched or hit my leg, I wouldn't feel it because the message doesn't get through my spinal cord and go to my brain. Because the message doesn't get to the brain, I don't feel the pain. See, everything starts in your brain. If you wiggle your fingers, it's because your brain sent a message to them to move. When you walk, your brain tells you to put one foot in front of the other one. If the spinal cord gets damaged and the message doesn't get through, the pain isn't felt.

After that description the hands go up. The questions from some elementary students have shocked me.

"What if I poured acid on your leg, would you feel it?"

I answered no and he laughed. "Cool!" he said.

"If I poured gasoline on your legs and then lit them on fire, you wouldn't feel it either?"

"No." And the kid sat there smiling. "I wouldn't feel it. But you'd be burning my leg, injuring my skin and muscles." The kid still smiled.

And another child, another day, asked, "You mean I could cut off your leg with a chain saw, you wouldn't feel it?"

And another asked what would happen if she hit my leg with a hammer or pounded a nail in it. The list goes on and gets much worse. Many children thought it would be cool if they could do those kinds of things to me.

The feeling in a group when those kinds of questions start, scares me. One question leads to another more horrific question. Think about your curiosity about violence and where it comes from. Think about how it affects your life.

Over the years a lot of kids have asked questions about life in a wheelchair and if it was fun being in a wheelchair. I always tell them I don't like the fact I have to use a wheelchair and how the electronics break down once in a while or it gets a flat tire at the worst possible time. But what I do like is the way I feel about myself now. I don't like the fact some people still stare or point at me. I don't like steps and doorknobs I can't grab onto because my hands don't work right. But I do like the feeling in my heart and in my head. You see, I concentrate on the positive things I can do, not on the negative things I can't do.

When kids ask me if it is fun being in a wheelchair, I tell them, "No, it's not fun, but I have fun in my chair." I have fun visiting schools and going for walks with a friend, or going to a movie. I have fun taking pictures with my cameras and watching my favorite sport – college basketball. I live in Minneapolis, Minnesota and have had front row seats since 1976 to watch the University of Minnesota's

Golden Gophers play basketball. That is what gets me through the Minnesota winters!

Kids ask me if I ever get bored. I can honestly say I never get bored, I have lots of things to do to keep myself busy learning and growing and changing every day. I recently got hooked up to the internet and I'm finding it to be my next big challenge. It is truly amazing to think about getting information instantly from all over the world. I know what you're thinking, "How does he type on the computer?" I have a small Velcro cuff fitted on my hand with a short pencil tucked into it with the eraser end out. I then hunt and peck with the eraser of the pencil and hit the keys. The mouse I kind of fumble with but I manage to make it work.

One day an eighth grader, in front of his whole school of about seven hundred students asked me, "If you could go back and play football again, would you?"

I asked him, "Do I know I'm going to get hurt?"

"Yes," he said.

"No I wouldn't, I'd have gone out for cross country."

He thought for a moment. "I'm glad you can't go back." he said.

"Because if you hadn't gotten hurt then you wouldn't be here with us today!"

COOL! That was a moment I'll never forget. It really made me feel good. I looked at him with a big smile on my face. "But maybe I would be your teacher or your coach."

You are all growing and changing every day. You are just beginning to develop your own special personality that will make you unique. You are developing a foundation on which your whole life will be built. Make that foundation strong and build a good life for yourself by learning to ask questions and act appropriately on the information you get from those questions. Remember there are no bad questions, the only bad ones are the ones that never get asked. "Think about it!"

# One More Tri

by
TONY SCHILLER

# One More Tri

by
### TONY SCHILLER

They were packed like sardines into the gym. 600 elementary school kids excited to hear me speak, or at least to get out of class. When their principal announced that the speaker was a world champion triathlete, a little girl in the front shouted, "What's a triathlete?" A third grade boy screamed back, "Someone who's <u>trying</u> to become an athlete?"

He knew that the <u>tri</u> in triathlete stood for three (as in the three sports which make up a triathlon race – swimming, cycling, and running), but like every great class clown, he just couldn't pass up an opportunity to make everyone laugh. It worked and the whole place cracked up.

They laughed because it was funny.
I laughed because it was true.

Wanting to be a great athlete more than anything, I spent most of my youth trying to become one. I tried all the sports, basketball, baseball, football and hockey, and always found myself struggling to keep up with the other kids.

As many kids grew in junior high, so too did my struggles. The best athletes got bigger, faster, and stronger and some even started shaving. Me? I got heavier all right, but it was mostly in the butt and gut and I sure didn't have use for a razor blade. With each new failure, I felt more self-conscious and gave more thought to giving up.

If you've had similar struggles, this story can help you find the strength to keep going. After all, it's true that I did turn things around from those days of desperately trying to become an athlete. In fact, I've now won over 100 races, including 3 gold medals from world triathlon championship races held in New Zealand, Mexico, and the United States.

I don't say this to brag or to pat myself on the back, but to use myself as an example of what's possible for you. My story will make three points that I believe are true:

#1. You have at least one special gift or talent in life.
#2. It might take you years of trying and failing to discover and develop it.
#3. You must have blind faith that all the hard work will be worth it.

Unfortunately, most people – even some with supreme talent – aren't willing to try long enough or hard enough. My best friends TJ and Bobby proved that. They had always been standout athletes despite never practicing very hard. Their laziness caught up with them in 9th grade when they lost their starting positions in basketball. After much whining and complaining, both stormed off the team in the middle of the season. I remember they blamed it on the coaches but it was their own fault.

Replacing basketball with a bad attitude, they took up cigarettes to look cool and started hanging out with the drug crowd and getting high. They put pressure on me to quit sports and join them. They told me that their new group of friends would accept me, and that I'd always be just a loser to the jocks.

Part of me was tempted to join them, not for the drugs, but for the friendship. I never did because deep inside I knew it was wrong for me. TJ and Bobby had quit on themselves. I have a saying, **beware of a quitter for they have nothing to lose by dragging you down with them**. Quitters will always welcome you in so they can feel better about their own bad decisions.

Once TJ and Bobby quit sports, they began to quit a lot of things. They quit being drug free, they quit trying in school, they quit having dreams for their future, and they even quit obeying the law. They taught me that quitting is never the answer. Quitting only makes it easier for you to quit again and again. So remember, **the worst time to quit is the first time**.

Though it was hard to watch two friends fall so far, it would have been much worse to have fallen with them.

Breaking away took courage and left me feeling very lonely, but it was a decision that changed my life.

While TJ and Bobby went downhill, I decided to give sports one more try. This time I went out for the track team with hopes of finally earning a junior high letter. My coach signed me up to run the mile the very next night in a 9th grade meet. Lining up to race I was so nervous that I almost wet my pants. Believe it or not, wearing high top Converse All-Stars, I took third place. Not bad, of course, there were only 2 others in the race. Embarrassed and exhausted, I crossed the finish line ready to quit sports once and for all.

That soon changed. My coach exclaimed, "Great job Tony!" I responded, "How do 'ya figure? I got last place." "That doesn't matter, you had a great time for your first race." Then he said, "I'm proud of you Tony. It took a lot of guts to come out here and race. It would have been a lot easier for you to be a coward and just hang out getting stoned with your buddies TJ and Bobby."

Shocked by his words, I asked how he knew about them and he said, "I just do. They're not fooling anyone." I laughed to myself and felt great that for the first time in my life a coach had said he was proud of me. Suddenly, the pain from the race was gone. I asked, "Coach, do you think I can beat those guys if I get a pair of spikes?" He answered, "Nope. Not by buying spikes you won't. But…

if you're really willing to commit yourself to running, well sure, you can do it...**someday.**"

Racing home, I told my parents their son had decided his calling was to be "A Runner!" With a tone of skepticism in their voice, they said, "That's nice." They probably figured this too will pass, but for the first time in my life I had a purpose that wasn't going to go away. **The road to someday began that day**.

Unfortunately, it was a very, very long road. That fall I joined one of the best high school cross country teams in the state only to become one of their slowest runners. Rather than being discouraged, I figured it was better to be among the worst on a great team than to be the best on a lousy team.

Making a deal with myself that no one on the team would ever beat me by outworking me, I became our most dedicated runner. I even started keeping a journal (diary) of my daily runs and races. The journal motivated me to run everyday just so I could write it down. For a long time it didn't seem like much, but eventually, my journal became an important part of my training.

And so like Forrest Gump, I ran...and ran...and ran... everyday, no matter what. Through all of Minnesota's coldest and hottest weather, I never missed a day. Soon it was 100 days, then 200, then 365, then 730, and past 1000 days with nearly 10,000 miles. Some kids in school admired my commitment. Others just thought anyone who ran that much must be weird. I figured, what the heck, they thought I was weird before I started running, so what's the difference now?

Although running 1000 straight days was physically grueling, the hardest part was waiting for all the hard work to pay-off. My progress was far slower than several teammates who ran half as much. Some even took their entire summers and winters off and still beat me. It didn't seem fair that they had so much talent and I had so little.

Through all the struggles, my coach kept saying to me, "Hard work always wins in the end. Your desire will take you so much further than their talent will ever take them." That was all I needed to keep going but it took thousands of miles before any real signs of success appeared. It's what you call doing something in **blind faith**. Finally, in my third year of running, the potential started catching up with the desire and I became competitive.

As I caught and surpassed my teammates, some gave excuses for losing to me and tried to distract me from my goals. It's not that they were bad people or that they didn't like me, it's just that it was hard for them to look at me and not see what they might have become. Like TJ and Bobby had done before them, they taught me an important lesson about human nature. <u>It's easier to hope others who are really committed fail than it is to make the same commitment yourself</u>.

You too will have friends who will be threatened by your commitment and you'll need to be strong not to let them distract you from your dreams. Is it worth it? Absolutely. You'll probably have your doubts (as I did all through junior and senior high) and that's when you'll need to have blind faith. Your blind faith will lead you to discovering and developing your natural talent.

Today, I meet many kids who say, "I'm just a hard worker and don't have natural talent." I tell them not to say that because it's simply not true. The ability to really commit yourself with blind faith to a long term goal is a talent. After all, most people can't do it. If you can, it's one of your talents!

But I believe each of us was born to be more than just a hard worker. We each have unique traits or skills that, if discovered and developed, can take us far. I was born with a remarkably strong heart and big lungs which top the list for what makes a good triathlete. Those traits are at the bottom of the list for what a baseball or football player needs.

Maybe, like I did as a kid, you've been trying activities or sports that don't fit well with your natural talents. Maybe you're trying to make your talent fit into the activities that are best for your friends. Maybe it's time for you to try something new. It's not quitting if you truly decide to switch and commit to something that suits you better. It might be in a new sport or a new activity. Who knows? It could even be that your special talent is best suited for something that hasn't been invented yet.

Such was the case for me. The sport of triathlon didn't even exist until after I graduated from college. It wasn't until I was 27 years old and **tried a tri** that I discovered my true calling as an athlete. My 180 pound frame had always been a big disadvantage for running. The opposite was true in triathlons where my size was an advantage for swimming and cycling which require strength. In no time at all I went from being one of the best runners in my state, to being one of the best triathletes in the world. And so the guy who had spent so many years trying to become an athlete, finally made it as a triathlete.

I'm glad it worked out this way too because racing triathlons is so exciting. When the gun goes off and hundreds of racers make a mad dash into the lake or ocean, it looks like a shark feeding frenzy. Reaching the shore after an intense mile or longer swim race is always a great feeling. We sprint right to our $4000 bikes (yep, you read that right) and take off without resting. I love the bike portion, especially going down mountain passes at over 60 mph, and averaging near 30 mph for the whole ride. Of course, there's still a run to complete and that's the toughest part because it's last and we don't hold anything back. My favorite part of a triathlon is finishing, and each finish makes me feel lucky today that I never gave up long ago as a kid.

# Chapter 11

# A Blueprint For Life

by
HEATHER SCHULTZ

## Pre TEEN POWER

# A Blueprint For Life

by

## Heather Schultz

I f you had the attention of millions of your peers what would you say? What would you want your message to be?

World Peace? Great idea, but I'm not in the mood.

Drug abuse? Yeah, but in 2500 words that could be pretty difficult.

*Why* do people use drugs? As in the words of Oprah, "That's a whole other show."

Violence? No, I'm afraid I'd leave you depressed and hopeless.

Then I heard a little voice in my head (I've had this checked out and the doctors say it's not a problem) say, "popularity."

Stop and ask yourself:

> *What* are you doing to be popular?

> *What* are you changing?

> *Who* are you changing? Yourself?

OK, stop reading this book. Go find a piece of paper and a pencil. Are you back yet? Let's get started. I want you to make a list of your values and beliefs that are most important to you. What kind of person do you want to be? Decide what you are not willing to compromise in the name of popularity. This will serve as your blueprint for life. A blueprint is something an architect uses to build a house, but we're going to use ours to build a future.

I was lucky because I figured out the meaning of popularity early in life. It all started in the fourth grade. I was very popular. Everyone liked me and wanted to be my friend. Life was great! But things can change in the blink of an eye. Even for a fourth grader.

My mom picked me up after school. She explained that dad had had a massive heart attack and needed open heart surgery. He was in the hospital near death. No, not my dad! This couldn't be the same dad who coached my basketball team, threw me high into the air and always managed to catch my squirming body, or tickled me til' I peed my pants. No, there was some mistake.

I closed my eyes and made a wish. "Please God, make my dad OK!"

When I opened my eyes nothing had changed!

Hey, wait a minute! Wishes are supposed to come true. Prayers are supposed to be answered.

But mine were not.

My dad's surgery went well and several weeks later he returned home. He was thin and frail, but still my dad, the man who would (and could) move heaven and earth for me. Several months later, my father decided he wanted to move closer to his family. His sister and brother lived about an hour away from us. So that year we moved to a new town, new school and new friends.

Hey, wait a minute. Did someone say new friends? I liked my old friends and they liked me.

Yeah, in the blink of an eye, life sure can change even for a fourth grader.

This new school wasn't so bad.

On the first day, a girl named Patti invited me to come over after school and hang out together. We became best friends, and soon I had lots of friends as many as I did at my old school. **Everyone** liked me. All the girls wanted to get their hair cut like mine. The "feathered" look was happening (ask your mom about it). I made the boys' list of the top 10 cutest girls. Fifth and sixth grade came and went and life was great. But in the blink of an eye, things can change even for a seventh grader.

A new year is always an exciting time. On the first day of seventh grade, this boy named Tom decided that he didn't like me. And even worse, he didn't want anyone else to like me. He was very popular. All the boys wanted to be as good at sports as he was, and all the girls wanted to date him. How could I compete with that!

Here is how that tragic day began.

It was before school and everyone was hanging out in the student lounge before class. The girls sat around gossiping. The boys, well, they were in their own little world. I was late to school that day (I always wondered if I had been a little later, maybe this wouldn't have gone down like this). Everyone was already in the lounge sitting in their usual spots.

As I crossed the room, Tom walked toward me.

Not thinking anything was wrong, I smiled and said, "hi."

But he just glared at me and yelled very loudly, "Leave, Heather. Get out of here!"

I felt a lump in my throat and I couldn't swallow.

Refusing to believe that this could actually be happening to me, I just laughed.

"No, Heather. I'm not joking. No one likes you here. Leave." Tom yelled.

I was scared.

I was embarrassed.

I was hurt.

I looked around, hoping someone would burst out laughing and yell, "PSYCHE!" I wanted someone to jump up and scream, "Joke, we gotcha!" Even if it wasn't a funny joke. Anything was better than what I was feeling. But no one did. A few looked away, knowing that they were wrong. But this was Tom, the most popular boy in school. Soon the whole room was chanting, "Leave, leave, leave." I slowly backed out, still hoping this was a joke.

I acted like nothing was wrong. I don't know who I was trying to convince. Myself or others.

I was sure this day would pass and tomorrow everything would be back to normal. Tomorrow, everyone would like me again.

*Have you ever been in a similar situation where you knew what was going down was wrong and hurtful? What did you do? Did you join in or did you stand up against it? I believe that in the student lounge that day, there were others who didn't want to join in. But they found themselves chanting along.*

*It is scary to go against the crowd.*

*Now think about **your** blueprint.*

- *What kind of a person do you want to be?*

- *How would you have handled that situation?*

- *Would you have confronted Tom?*

- *Would you have walked out of the student lounge?*

- *Would you have joined in with the chanting?*

- *Will you join the crowd regardless of how it makes some-one else feel?*

The next morning, I stood outside the student lounge. I took a deep breath and walked in, smiling and pretending yesterday never happened. Everyone look at me in amazement. I don't know if they thought I was brave or stupid.

A hush fell over the room as Tom approached me. All eyes were on Tom and me.

"I thought I told you yesterday. Leave, Heather. No one likes you!"

Once again I left.

For the next two years of my life I was mostly alone. Patti, my best friend, never left my side. I tried to hang-out with the popular kids. Sitting in the same bleachers at sporting events, walking together in the halls, but I was always a few steps behind. Everyone knew I wasn't <u>really</u> accepted. And I knew it, too.

At lunch I always sat at the "popular" table even though no one ever talked to me except if I was lucky enough to sit by Patti. I remember one day when Patti was absent from school. I sat down at the "popular" table and at the same time **everyone** got up and moved to another table.

I wanted to escape. To someone or something.

But, it was just me, this cold cafeteria table and that same old question, "Why me?" I wanted to be popular again. But how? I was willing to do anything.

*Do you know someone at your school who sits alone everyday? Who walks alone down the hall with their eyes on the floor and no smile? Who never gets asked to hang out? These people may feel alone, unaccepted. You can change that! By reaching out to these people you may change they way they feel about themselves. Try to practice "for no good reason" an act of kindness everyday of your life.* **Think** *of others and* **do** *for others. Just because you know it's the right thing to do. Take the time to say hello, or smile, sit and talk with someone new. It's the small and thoughtful acts we do each day that can make the difference between someone liking or disliking themselves.*

In the beginning of eighth grade, Patti and I decided to have a party. It was at my house. I knew people would come because Patti was still popular. And I was right. Every popular person was in **my** basement! I thought things had changed for me. Maybe people liked me again. Maybe I was popular again. But a boy named Todd brought me back to reality. Everyone was playing the kissing game, Spin-the-Bottle. Todd spun the bottle and it landed on me. That meant we had to go into the closet and kiss one time. Well, I couldn't have been happier. Todd was really cute and I felt popular again. We walked into the closet and pulled the door shut. Just Todd and I in a dark closet. I puckered up my lips and shut my eyes but the silence was broken by Todd's words, "You know, I don't really want to kiss you. Let's just count to 10 and tell the others that we did."

**10-9-8** "Please change your mind!" I prayed.
**7-6-5** "Someone save me." I pleaded.
**4-3-2** "Why me?" I asked.
**1.**

Things can change even in a few short seconds.

By the end of my eighth grade, Tom was getting bored picking on me. He had lost interest in his quest to depopularize me. Even though he had succeeded.

It was now the summer before high school. A new beginning. A chance to be popular again. I did a lot of thinking and soul-searching that summer. It took me two long, hurtful years to understand the importance of popularity. What's popular, what's cool and what's in can change in a blink of an eye. But people don't. I was still me. A little wiser now but still the same seventh grade girl who entered that student lounge and never went back. But still me.

I decided to enter high school with a new attitude. Popularity <u>wasn't</u> to die for. I was going to do what made **me** happy. If people liked me, great. But first, I had to like me. And you know what? People did like me. And I was respected. I went on to be voted class president, most likely to succeed, homecoming court and outstanding senior girl. I was a cheerleader, basketball player and I had friends. Everyday I sat with different people at a different cafeteria table and I walked down the hallway with anyone I wanted, <u>not who I wanted to be seen with.</u> I didn't care if I was the most popular person. I lived for me and for what I knew was right and moral. I was true to my blueprint.

I haven't told many people about my seventh and eighth grade years. I guess I was too embarrassed. But now I know that those two years helped define who I am today and what is important to me. During my high school years, Tom came by my house and apologized for what he had done. I guess he is a little wiser now. I know I am.

In some ways popularity can be defined as peer pressure. Think about different pressure situations you may find yourself in. What is your game plan? It will be easier to handle a tough situation if you know how to react ahead of time. You will be able to think clearly and make better decisions if you're not under pressure to decide on the spot.

Think about the issues that you and your friends face every day for the sake of being "popular."

*DRUG USE:* The number one reason young people say they do drugs is peer pressure. To fit in. To be popular. They <u>think</u> everyone is doing it. The fact is: One in four teenagers uses an illegal drug. That is alarming! But it also means 3 out of 4 teenagers are **not** using drugs. So everyone is *not* doing it. As a motivational speaker, I travel across the world and I meet more young people who are **not** doing drugs. Young people who are outgoing, athletic, intelligent and yes...popular. Doing drugs may kill you, but it won't make you popular.

*GANGS & VIOLENCE:* Some young people join gangs because they want to belong and they need people who will accept them and make them feel popular. Many gangs today are involved with illegal and dangerous behavior. Some gangs make you go through an initiation to prove your loyalty. This may include dealing drugs, robbery and even murder. Most gangs have a "jump-in" initiation where current gang members beat you for one full minute! Having a group of friends to hang out with is OK. But not if you are pressured to do things that go against your beliefs, compromise your values or are dangerous and illegal.

*CHEAT, LIE & STEAL:* Has anyone ever wanted to copy your homework or cheat off your test paper? Have you ever known that someone was doing something wrong and lied to cover up for them? These are **really** tough situations. You can avoid these types of pressure situations by choosing your friends wisely. Don't hang out with people who would ask you to cheat, steal or lie. A true friend would not want to put you and your safety at risk. **Cheating, stealing or lying will not make you popular!** It only makes you a cheater, a liar and a thief.

Don't put yourself, your safety, your character or your integrity at-risk just to be popular.

A few years ago, I went to my 10th year class reunion from high school. It was great to see everyone, even Tom. But that night popularity was once again defined for me. No one could remember who dated who, who was a cheerleader, who was the quarterback, who was prom queen or who was even popular. But we did remember who was nice, kind and whom we respected.

Please, look at your life. Ask yourself these questions: How important is popularity to you? What are you doing in the name of popularity? Who or what are you changing? Can you say, "I like me, not because others do, but because *I* like me." Because in the blink of an eye, everything can change. Stick to your blueprint of beliefs. Remember, what right isn't always what's popular and what's popular isn't always what's right.

You've got your blueprint and your tools. Start building!

# The Champion, Wanna-Be, and Spectator in You

by
CAMI C. VEIRE, MS

# The Champion, Wanna-Be, and Spectator in You

by
CAMI C. VEIRE, MS

A young man walked down the bleachers to where I was standing after speaking about overcoming obstacles in life. He hung back while others thanked me for my message and for coming to their school. It was obvious he wanted to share something with me. After everyone else was on their way back to class, he approached.

"Cami," he said, "may I ask you a question?"

"Sure."

He took one gentle step back and opened his arms, looked down his body and then back up at me.

"Do I look like a jock?"

I was on the spot. "You know what?" I responded. "You have really caught me off guard. I'm not into labeling people by what I see and you have asked me to do that."

"That's cool," he said. "You won't offend me by your answer. I'm only trying to make a point."

I stepped back. I saw a young man with hair down to the middle of his back, an earring, black jeans, black t-shirt, black motorcycle jacket, and black work boots.

"Do I look like a jock?" he asked again.

"No man, you don't," I responded nervously. Quickly and boldly Mike made his point.

"Cami, I appreciated that part of your presentation to our school, you know that part where you talked about finding the 'Champion' inside of you, and that you don't have to be athletic, or termed a jock, to fit in. Well, I am not athletic or a jock – I like to tinker under the hoods of automobiles. You can find me hanging around at my grandfather's gas station, or when I am in school, you can find me hanging around in the shop.

"But you know what, I don't get my name in the school newspaper, and I don't get recognized in the local newspaper. The only time I get recognized is when there is trouble at school. Then they blame me and my friends, no matter what. But I love being a mechanic and will be the best mechanic this city has ever had when I graduate. In fact, I bet I can fix a car better than a mechanic with ten years of professional experience."

He had absolute confidence in his abilities to be successful. I knew he would be.

"Thanks for recognizing all of us – not just the jocks. Thanks for looking beyond how I choose to dress and the length of my hair. Thanks for telling my friends that we can be successful just like everyone else."

Mike the Champion walked away.

This chapter is your gentle reminder that you are a special person with many abilities. You have hopes and dreams. You have the energy and enthusiasm to make your dreams become reality. You can do anything you put your mind, heart, and life into! You can make positive things happen in your life!

I have just reminded you how great you are. You know that. **BUT** ...

Then there's **Life** – it really throws us for a loop sometimes. Things happen that we don't expect...we handle problems and confrontations in a way that we wished we had not...we get frustrated, stressed, and maybe even depressed. All of us want to get back to feeling in control – of thinking, believing, and living life with a positive attitude and giving our very best to every encounter and responsibility we have. Don't quit!  Say **"I CAN!"**

Remember – you have a Champion inside of you!

## The Champion In You

Sarah is a seventh grader who starts on the varsity basketball team in her small rural school. Since fourth grade she has attended numerous summer basketball camps and has worked hard to be a great basketball player. Her success at an early age prompted jealousy from older kids. They harassed her younger brother. They pressured her to break the rules, to drink, and to do other things that would make her ineligible to play varsity basketball and jeopardize her college career.

Sarah's hard work had prepared her for challenges on the court. Now she faced challenges off the court. She could face them like a Champion, or she could fold and quit. What would you choose?

Sarah chose to be a Champion. She didn't give in to peer pressure to drink and break rules. She never lost sight of her goal and her dream – to play college basketball. Sarah continued to practice hard and focus on her talents and abilities rather than let negative peer pressure take control of her decision making power.

Sarah was a little girl when her mother, in a caring voice, told her about monsters and kisses. Sarah still remembers that conversation, and it helps her keep a Champion attitude.

"Sarah, there are monsters out there who will eat you up if you let them. Not like the monsters you see in scary movies. Rather, people. People will act like monsters and try to make you do things you know are not right – they will try to gobble you up so that you come down to their level. You see Sarah, there are people in this world that will be jealous of you and want you to quit achieving your goals."

"What do I do with these monsters, Mom?"

"You reach out and kiss them gently on the end of their noses."

"What do you mean, kiss them gently on the end of their noses?"

"You continue to excel, work hard, stay focused on your goals and dreams, and never stoop to the monsters' level and play their game. You never hit back. Instead, you walk away and try to work things out at the appropriate time. You continue to reach out to people with your uplifting smile, kind words, and deeds. You continue to share your enthusiasm and positive attitude about life with everyone, even the monsters that try to bring you down.

"That is how you kiss those monsters gently on the end of their noses, Sarah. Show them that their harassment will not work with you. You are a Champion, Sarah, and Champions never quit!"

We all have a Champion inside of us. Not the type of champion that crosses the finish line first, but a Champion with an attitude like Mike and Sarah's. They faced adversity, but never lost sight of their dreams and goals. They didn't give in to peer pressure. Mike was himself; he didn't feel he had to be a jock to succeed. Sarah didn't give in to pressures to drink or to pick a fight when her brother was being harassed.

What else do Champions do? Champions make mistakes! They take risks knowing that they will make mistakes. To them, it's okay to make mistakes: they learn and grow from them.

Champions also take responsibility for their actions. Champions look you in the eye and say "I'm sorry" when they are wrong. They don't blame others when they are responsible.

Lisa, a sixth grader, told me about a Champion decision …

"My friend Sue and I were making plans for the weekend. We decided that we wanted to have a sleep over, just the two of us. Normally we chummed around with our other friend, Sally. Sally was hurt when she saw Sue and I making plans and she was not included.

"I had a choice to make," Lisa said. "I could continue making plans with Sue and ignoring Sally, or I could go up to Sally and say, 'I'm sorry for ignoring you,' and include her in our plans."

Lisa chose to apologize to her friend. It takes guts to admit you are wrong. It takes courage to say "I'm sorry." A

Champion, like Lisa, has guts and courage.

How else can you spot a Champion? They don't gossip. They go out of their way to say something positive about a person who is being put down by others.

*You have a Champion inside of you!*

## The Wanna-Be In You!

Ben, an eighth grader, shared his story....

"Cami, I really want to get good grades in school but I just can't. I really want to take good care of myself by showering every day, wearing clean clothes, and combing my hair, but I just can't. Gee, I wish I could be like Johnny. He is so cool. He gets good grades, looks nice, and all the girls just love him.... I wish I could be like Johnny."

I asked him about his study habits. He had a difficult time listening to his teachers and he never took his books home to do his homework or to study. Yet he wanted good grades.

To get an extra 20 minutes of sleep, he would skip showering. He would roll out of bed, not even bothering to comb his hair or put a clean clothes before he arrived at school, barely on time. Yet he wanted to feel good and look nice.

He thought he had a lot of friends because when he put people down and talked about other people behind their backs, people would laugh. But at lunch time, no one wanted to sit by him. Yet he wanted to be like Johnny and have lots of friends and have the girls love him.

I want.......

I want........

I want.......

You have to be willing to work to get what you want! You do not become a great student by putting in your time at school each day. You become a great student by taking your books home and challenging yourself above and beyond what your teachers challenge you in the classroom. You do not become a great athlete by showing up for a two hour practice every day with the coach. You become a great athlete by enhancing your skills when the coach is not around. You attend camps, lift weights, train, and more.

Yet Wanna-Be's are content with just doing what they have to do to get by. They join in when others are being put down because they don't feel good about themselves. They are quick to blame. Wanna-Be's need to look in the mirror and take care of number one.

*Be careful! You have a Wanna-Be inside of you!*

## The Spectator Inside of You

When I was growing up a certain individual attended every athletic event. He would take his same seat at each home game and occasionally travel to away games that were close to home. Spectator is defined as an "onlooker." He was a true spectator in the sense of the word.

Let's look at being a spectator in life. When we spectate we choose to "look on." There is little, if any, effort in our actions. Our thoughts about self and others tend to be disrespectful; enthusiasm and energy for what we do is low; and our attitudes need adjusting. When there is an opportunity to gossip or put others down, as spectators we are usually the instigators or always involved in the act. We want things in life but are not willing to work for them. It is simply easier to sit back and watch – to spectate – and let others do the work. If others do not do the work to our liking, we will be the first to put them down.

*You have a Spectator inside of you!*

## It's Your Choice. Choose To Be a Champion!

Every second and every hour of every day, life is full of choices.

Life is a roller coaster ride! It is scary, bumpy, makes your tummy feel funny, turns you upside down and sideways, goes fast and slow, and will come to a complete stop. When you ride the roller coaster of life, remember that you will make mistakes along the way – you are not perfect. You need to get back in that roller coaster seat and place that safety bar across your shoulders. Hang on! Do your very best with the situations that will come your way.

Life is also challenging! Encounter obstacles and situations with a positive attitude. Learn from your mistakes rather than blaming others. In the long run, you will feel better about yourself and treat others like you want to be treated.

I bet you rarely have speakers come into your school and tell you to make mistakes. I tell my audiences to make mistakes! Then I challenge them to see mistakes in a positive way and learn from them. Accept responsibility and move on. That is the only way you grow as a positive person – make mistakes! Look at them, learn from them! Make mistakes!

Remind yourself, "If it is to be – it is up to me!" You choose who you are. The ultimate goal for everyone is to stay in that **Champion** category as much as we can.

We also have to get real: we have challenges in life that bring us down. We may fall into a **Wanna-Be** mode and forget we have abilities and energies to create our own happiness and grow our self esteem. If we chose to let the negative thoughts completely take over, we may become **Spectators.** We'll blame others, instead of taking responsibility. We'll spend time gossiping, instead of constructively working towards goals and dreams.

With every challenge, we have a choice about how we will react to that challenge, how we will deal with that challenge, and what we will learn from that challenge.

*Face challenges as a Champion!*

# Think It, Believe It, Live It!

Go out and make your life great! You can do anything you put your mind and your heart into. Remember Mike, the young man with the long hair, earring, and black clothes from head to toe. He truly believed in himself and his love for auto mechanics. Even though his school and society do not recognize him because he is not in a clique that gets a lot of recognition, he knows in his heart he will be successful.

Remember Sarah, the basketball player who remained focused on her goals when monsters tried to sidetrack her with harassment, put-downs, and negative pressures. There is a true Champion inside Sarah – and there is a true Champion inside of you! Don't let Wanna-Be's and Spectators enter your life. Give your Champion attitude plenty of practice so it becomes the first attitude you reach for when you're faced with obstacles, challenges, and tough decisions.

### I encourage you: never stop dreaming!

This simple formula works for everyone who really wants it to work....

- Have a positive mental attitude (THINK IT) ,
- Have enthusiasm for everything you do in life (BELIEVE IT),
- Have a daily approach that encourages you to remain focused on your vision and see your dreams become reality (LIVE IT).

## DARE TO DREAM BIG DREAMS!

IT IS NOT WHAT'S ON THE OUTSIDE THAT
MATTERS – IT IS ONLY WHAT'S ON THE INSIDE
THAT MATTERS.

I wish you happiness as you

search for, find, and keep that

**Champion** inside of you!

# Don't Be Extraordinary

by
C. KEVIN WANZER

Pre
TEEN
POWER

Don't be extraordinary. Be extra-unique.

Sometimes, it seems as if people are more interested in finding fault with a person rather than looking for their good qualities. Your student body at school may be like that, too. If somebody drops his tray in the lunch room, what happens? Well, duh. Of course it falls to the ground. But what else? You got it. People clap and cheer. Not everybody, but some do. How many people jump from their comfortable chairs to go and help that person? Sadly, very few. A true student leader helps without giving it a second thought, regardless of the consequences.

Make sure that you are striving to be the person you truly want to be. Not what your parents, teachers or friends want you to be...what *you* want to be. Remember that some outside influences can lead you down a path you never wanted to walk in the first place. Simply ask yourself, "Am I able to look up to myself as a positive role model and follow my true dreams?" (Just don't ask it out loud.) Hopefully, your answer is YES! Your inner voice will guide you. Listen.

I was speaking in a school once, when halfway through my presentation the fire alarm went off. We had to evacuate the building because of some law that says you cannot be in a school and voluntarily get burned. (I guess they really *don't* want you to smoke in school.) Sure enough it was a true alarm. Smoke from a science lab set it off. No big deal. No real harm done. "Better safe than charred," is what I always say. Then I thought, wouldn't it be cool if we all had an internal alarm system that went off right before something bad happened to us. And I realized we do – it is called indigestion.

No, no, no silly. It is called your instinct.

That weird little alarm and feeling inside that helps guide you along in life is your instinct. Your instinct will always guide you in the right direction. But you have to practice using it. Like anything, if you stop practicing you start to get rusty. It is when people ignore their instinct all together that they run the risk of losing their conscience, morals and values. Although there are a great deal of issues that you will face through your journey of the teenage years, I have chosen to focus on three opportunities in which your instinct will help lead you down the right road. Your happiness all depends on your decision to break the norm and be extra-unique.

## DIVERSITY...
### We Are All Just Jelly Beans

Look at the cover of this book. Go ahead. Look at it. Did you do it? Good. Isn't it cool owning a scratch and sniff book? Go ahead and try it.* Now take the book and waive it frantically above your head screaming, "Look at me, I am reading! Yippee!" Did you do that? Great. You really *are* abnormal. Cool. Now, look at the cover again. Pretty sweet isn't it? (Pun intended.) What do you notice about it? "Ummm...they are all jelly beans." Well, that is good my sweet-tooth friend. What I was really looking for was the fact that the jelly beans are a lot like what we are going through in life...a whole bunch of us all thrown together into a big jar. More importantly, notice all the colors. They are all just floating around in the jelly bean jar of life. And jelly beans could care less what color each one is. Probably because they can't see. Also, chances are when you are a jelly bean, you don't want to be the most popular color because you are more likely to get eaten! Jelly beans simply exist to please you without judging each other.

Chances are you don't have a bowl of jelly beans available. However, if you were to close your eyes and touch them, they would all feel the same. Kinda' like when you close your eyes, all people look the same. Isn't it funny how so much of prejudice is based on appearance? How many blind people are prejudice toward others just because of their looks? Probably not many. You don't really know what a jelly bean is like until you bite into it and start chewing. The same goes with friendships and accepting others. Until you really "bite" into a person and take the time to know and understand them, you won't really know what they are like. Now, I am not suggesting that you start munching on your friends. (Unless, of course, you are Mike Tyson. He is so EARie. When he fought Evander Holyfield, he really bit off more than he could chew. Maybe he just wanted a real cool souvenEAR.)

The truth is, you don't really know someone until you actually *experience* that person. You have to take the time to get to know what that person is all about...what makes him tick. Until then, it is dangerous to develop an opinion about him. Your natural born instinct tells you to accept others unconditionally. After all, people are not born prejudice. It is a learned behavior. Prejudice is ignorance. What's your IQ?

## ALCOHOL AND OTHER DRUGS...
### "Be-Wiser-er" Than Your Buds

Mothers Against Drunk Driving created a t-shirt that showed three squished frogs on the side of the road after getting "smashed" by alcohol. I love that shirt. It is an effective way of getting across a serious message in a fun way. By now you have probably heard enough drug lectures to last a lifetime. I know they can be kinda' repetitive and boring. Sometimes people talking about drugs are so boring, some kids want to start doing drugs just to get out of the lecture. The bottom line is that being drug-free is a choice you have to make *by* yourself...*for* yourself. No one can do it for you. But to be successful in being drug-free, there is one important thing you must have. Ammunition. (No, not bullets. Although that would be an effective way to stay drug-free, I don't want you to shoot anyone who offers you alcohol or other drugs.) I want you to 'arm' yourself with the knowledge as to why you want to be drug-free. In a word: education.

If someone were to ask a typical student, what the most dangerous drug in the world is, they would hear a variety of answers. Acid. Heroin. Angel Dust. But, in reality, the most dangerous drug is any drug a person is not scared to use himself. These are the gateway drugs. These are the drugs that, once you start using them, can "open the gate" to other drugs down the road. Alcohol, marijuana, tobacco and Doritos are the most dangerous drugs because most people are not afraid of their possible consequences. (Okay, maybe Doritos aren't drugs, but you have to admit they are addictive. They are kinda' like Pringles potato chips – once you pop, you can't stop.) The bottom line is that if you can resist the gateway drugs, chances are you will never become addicted to another drug. After all, not too many people start out using drugs hoping to become addicted. Most people are just in it for the high...the quick ride.

My promise to you is this. I guarantee that if you surround yourself with friends who believe and support your choice to stay drug-free...chances are you will stay drug-free. If your friends choose to use, chances are you will try drugs, too. Sometimes, your friends say more about you then you say about yourself. Choose them carefully. Your instinct tells you that you should avoid drugs. You know that. Pay attention to it and be proud of your choice to be drug-free.

# FOLLOW YOUR PASSION...
## Confucius Says, "Choose A Career You Love And You'll Never Work A Day In Your Life."

When you were a baby, what was your passion in life? It was all really simple. Smiling, laughing, sleeping and as you grew older, trying to hit the toilet (especially boys.) Your parents were so excited for you that they even video-taped your first bowel movements. How lovely. (Hopefully they do not do that anymore. That would be a whole different book titled, *PEE-TEEN POWER*.)

So, what is the one question you have been asked since you were a kid that some adults still ask today? No, it is not "Do you have to go potty?" It is that infamous question, "What do you want to be when you grow up?" Right from the beginning we are conditioned to believe that *who* you are is determined by *what* you are. Kinda' sad when you think about it. Instead the question should be "*Who* do you want to be when you grow up?" You should be measured by who you are and the goodness you bring toward others, rather than what you do for a living. Regardless of you career, you can always make the world a better place through your attitude and deeds.

The teenage years will be filled with choices, temptations but most importantly – FUN! However, start setting your sights now on what you would like to do as a career. Sadly, some people define who you are by your job not by you as a person. Consequently, some people get caught up following careers that *other people* want them to follow. When in reality, what they truly want to do is entirely different. Don't allow yourself to fall into that trap.

You have a passion, a true desire to pursue that tiny little dream in the back of your head. We all do. Go for it. One of my favorite quotes is, "Choose a job you love so much that you would do it for free. Then do it so well that somebody pays you for it." Again, your instinct can help determine what your true loves are. You don't have to decide today what you are going to do as a career for the rest of your life. After all, your passion can change day by day. Just make sure that as you travel through the teenage years, you get involved in the activities that you truly have a love for, not what someone else has a passion for and therefore expects you to. Regardless of what you do...in school...at home...or as a career...make sure that you are being true to yourself. Be real. So, after you take the *Preteen Power* journey, hopefully you will know the answer when someone asks you, "What do you want to be when you grow up?" You can look at them and say, "I want to be me. I want to be extra-unique." Your instinct will always lead you to your passion, but you must be willing to follow.

So, there you have it.

There are more than these three opportunities when following your instinct will be very helpful, but this is a pretty good start. The teenage years are going to be amazing.

Enjoy them. Savor them. Learn from them. And when you feel at times that you are the only one who is making positive choices, think about the fact that perhaps YOU are the one who is on track and the rest of the world is upside down.

*You didn't really try to scratch and sniff the cover did you? You did? Really. Wow. You really aren't extraordinary. Congratulations on being extra-unique.

# Who Wrote What and Why –
# *Meet the Authors*

## PreTEEN POWER

# KARL ANTHONY

### Who Really Cares

Over one million students know Karl Anthony and his music. Since 1984 he has toured the world including all fifty states in the U.S.A.

Karl Anthony has an uncanny ability to completely mesmerize an audience with his unpredictable and playful style promoting non-violence, cultural respect and healthy lifestyles.

Karl uses Humor, Group Interaction and Music with a Message to create the ultimate successful program.

FREE CATALOG OR PROMOTIONAL VIDEO..........Call 1-800-843-0165

P.O.Box 3064
Carlsbad, CA 92009
760-434-5554 fax 434-5596
800-843-0165
kaanthony@aol.com

---

# PHIL BOYTE

### Be Yourself – the Voices Scream
### *What Does That Really Mean?*

Phil works with schools who are creating a better place for students to learn and with kids who want to grow and have fun. Whether writing or speaking, Phil wants his audience to think. So many people talk about excellence but Phil is committed to it at every level. His presentations to teachers and students alike are full of stories, magic, and humor but the message challenges people to make a change in the way they live. Phil has several books available – *Focus – 36 Ten Minute Lesson Plans, Secrets of Fundraising,* and *The Student Body President Handbook*. Call Phil's office to order any of the above or to speak to him about speaking for your school or conference.

34599 Morgan Trail
Elizabeth, CO 80107
303-646-0505 fax 646-9821
800-874-1100
ASKPHIL@aol.com

## ERIC CHESTER

### We All Get Older...
### *But Not Everyone Grows Up!*

"You are, by far, the greatest speaker in the world!"

After his 13 year old son, Zac, finally admitted this to his father, he was let out of the refrigerator.

When he's not "horsing around" with his kids or teasing his wife, Eric Chester is out providing motivation, hope, inspiration, and usable ideas for a better life to pre-teens, teens, teachers, and parents. Since 1989, his original one-of-a-kind programs have been enjoyed by millions world wide. Eric is a former teacher, coach, and sports promoter, and is the player-coach of the popular Teen Power book series.

c/o TEEN POWER
1410 Vance St. - Ste. #201
Lakewood, CO 80215
303-239-9999 fax 239-9901
800-304-ERIC
ECSpeak@aol.com
www.ericchester.com

## JOHN CRUDELE

### Stand for Something...
### *or Fall for Anything*

Throughout the past 14 years, John's presented over 3,000 programs to more than one million people internationally. Popular with students and adults, John impacts school, conference and community audiences with life-changing messages, humorous insights and a powerful delivery style. His books *Making Sense of Adolescence: How to Parent From the Heart*, and his contributions to the *TEEN POWER* series unravel the mysteries of adolescence. He is a frequent guest on talk-radio and TV shows including the *Rikki Lake* and *Jenny Jones* shows. Youth and parent cassette programs are also available.

John Crudele
Speeches and Seminars
9704 Yukon Court
Minneapolis, MN 55438
612-942-6207 fax 942-7601
800-899-9KID
JCSpeak@aol.com

## M. K. DURAND FARLEY

### I Wanna Be a Muppet

M. K. Durand Farley is an entertainer, educator and motivator who has worked with many organizations including PRIDE, HBO and the National Association of School Resource Officers. This charismatic, enthusiastic, exciting, actor, singer, writer and musician speaks from the heart in an inspiring language we all understand. Since 1987 he has reached an audience of nearly 3 million with anti-drug and violence messages, leadership training and inciting activism. *"Why?"*…you may ask. *"Because it matters and because we must!"* Durand replies. His dedication, compassion and captivating presence has made him a memorable favorite of communities and conferences throughout the world.

Durand Speaks International
4008 Bayside Circle
Doraville, GA 30340
770-939-0034 (phone & fax)
e-mail: DuranSpeak@aol.com

## JENNIFER ESPERANTE GUNTER

### Life is a Roller Coaster…
### *Enjoy the Ride!*

Jennifer Esperante Gunter (also known as the Cha Cha Queen) gives hope to youth, teachers, and parents across America as a Keynote Speaker, Workshop Leader, and Mistress of Ceremonies. Through stories, humor, and entertainment, **Jennifer** encourages her audiences to make *healthy choices* focusing on *Self-Esteem, Values, Leadership, and Character Development.*

**Jennifer** is Miss Sonoma County 1992 and Miss San Francisco 1993. She has produced shows for the San Francisco 49ers and the Jeep Eagle Aloha Bowl and holds a degree in Psychology. **Jennifer** is the author of *Winning with the Right Attitude,* and co-author of the original TEEN POWER!

Gunter Productions
P.O. Box 8368
Santa Rosa, CA. 95407
fax 707-523-7047
800-357-6112
CHAQUEEN@AOL.COM

## NORM HULL

**It Takes GUTS to Make a Difference**

Norm first began speaking professionally to high school students in 1980. From the East Room of the White House to the halls of the Kremlin...from the frozen tundra of Alaska to the Department of Defense in his hometown of Washington D.C....Norm has worked with the motivation and leadership development of teenagers, educators, parents and corporate America. Norm will soon host "Beyond The Norm," a youth oriented television show now in pre-production. Write for more information on the programs Norm provides.

26440 Mapleridge Way
Moreno Valley, CA 92555
909-682-2020 fax 243-6825
AskNorm@aol.com

## DENNIS MITCHELL

**The Winning Difference!**

As a teen, Dennis was in and out of juvenile, gang banging, doing drugs, and eventually found himself on the Police Department's "Most Wanted" list.

Fate eventually caught up with Dennis and soon he found himself in another type of gang, a chain gang! While doing hard time, his 5-year-old son Little Dennis, was murdered by a drinking driver! This tragic event changed Dennis' life forever!

Success-N-Effect
Empowerment Seminars
9116 E. Sprague, Suite 66
Spokane, WA 99206
509-625-0299 fax 924-3668

After spending 8 1/2 years in the penitentiary, Dennis turned his life around and is now one of the country's most sought after dynamic speakers. He is the author of the book "Success You Can," and he produces audio tapes, designer T-shirts & baseball caps.

## MIKE PATRICK

### The Domino Theory

INCREDIBLE • INFORMATIVE • INSPIRING • IRREPRESSIBLE

Just ask his audience. Mike Patrick is a lot of positive adjectives, adjectives that will change and improve lives. Patrick, a quadriplegic since age 16 as a result of a football injury, is a health educator who converts limitations to achievements.

Mike's presentations help individuals overcome obstacles, creatively solve problems, affect attitudes, change perceptions and perform successfully. His message includes candor, wit and humor.

Mike Patrick is a realist. He says, I want young people to learn if you think things through, you can find a solution to just about any problem. The problem isn't the issue, the issue is how you deal with the problem.

Patrick Communications, Inc.
3225 Emerson Avenue South
Minneapolis, MN   55408-3523
612-827-4110   fax 824-9229
800-972-9537
mike@patcom.com
Web Site: www.patcom.com

## TONY SCHILLER

### One More Tri

Tony is a 3-time world champion in the grueling sport of triathlon. As an inspiring storyteller, he draws heavily from the lessons learned both as a struggling young athlete and as a world-class competitor. His gift as a speaker is his ability to connect with a wide range of audience types and ages. Tony is equally as effective working with troubled teens as he is with champion athletes. Since 1990, his BreakAway message has been presented at hundreds of K-12 schools and conferences on the keys to higher self esteem, confidence, and peak performance.

6580 Troendle Circle
Chanhassen, MN 55317
612-474-3278   fax 474-4527
800-863-3278
Trispeak@aol.com

## HEATHER SCHULTZ

### A Blueprint For Life

Heather Schultz, R.N. is one of the few speakers who can do it all! **SCHOOL ASSEMBLIES** that are direct and hard-hitting. Students leave wanting more. **KEYNOTE ADDRESSES** guaranteed to motivate and energize any audience. What a way to kick off or end any conference! Interactive **WORKSHOPS** which are fun and educational. **ADULT/PARENT/ TEACHER** presentations proven to empower, educate, and heighten awareness. Heather is a highly requested speaker who has over 10 years of experience. She has traveled the world sharing her message with millions!

2980 Appling Drive
Atlanta, GA 30341
770-936-8487
800-624-8939
SpeakPeace@AOL.com

School Assemblies • Conferences
Adult Presentations
Speaker • Educator • Motivator

## CAMI C. VEIRE, MS

### The Champion, Wanna-Be,
### and Spectator in You

*"It is in dreaming the greatest dreams....Seeking the highest goals...that we build the brightest tomorrow."*

Enthusiastic! Sincere! Spellbinding! These are words used to describe Cami C. Veire and her powerful presentations. Cami shares moving stories about young people she has met over the past 12 years as a counselor, trainer, athletic official, and friend. Cami invites her audiences to take a roller coaster ride with her as she explores challenges of life. Since 1990, Cami has encouraged youth across the United States and Canada to dream big dreams! Her topic areas include motivation, self-esteem, alcohol & other drugs, peer helping, and leadership. Cami lives with her husband Jeff and their three children in Sioux Falls, South Dakota.

CC & Associates
Professional Speaking & Training Firm
2209 Wellington Avenue S.
Sioux Falls, SD 57106-0549
605-361-7203 fax 336-2563
800-211-CAMI
imagery@iw.net

# C. KEVIN WANZER

### Don't Be Extraordinary

P.O. Box 30384
Indianapolis, IN 46230-0384
317-253-4242
800-4.KEVIN.W
justsayha@aol.com
http://members.aol.
com/justsayha

C. Kevin Wanzer has spoken in so many elementary, middle and high schools that he's lost count. (But then again, he only got a C in math.) Chances are, you've already experienced Kevin in your school or at a conference; he's the guy who used comedy to get across a pretty serious message. Kevin "edu-tains" about prejudice, drug education, personal excellence and leadership. If, for some reason, you haven't heard Kevin, you gotta' check him out! You'll remember him long after the laughter. Kevin dedicates his chapter to the newest pre-teen of his life, his beautiful niece, Anna Moreno.

---

### Other
# TEEN POWER

#### Books Available Through ChesPress

**TEEN POWER** *A Treasury of Solid Gold Advice for Today's Teens* from America's Top Youth Speakers, Trainers, and Authors.

**TEEN POWER TOO** *More Solid Gold Advice for Teens* from America's Top Speakers, Trainers, and Authors.

**TEEN EmPOWER** *Solid Gold Advice for Those Who Teach, Lead, and Guide Teens* from America's Top Speakers and Authors in Education.

---

# "If I could do it all over again, I'd...."

## Reflections from
### "EXPERIENCED" TEENS

# "If I could do it all over again, I'd...."

### Reflections from
### "Experienced" Teens

E ach of us only gets "one shot" at life as a teenager. You often get advice from adults who tell you what they would do if they "had it to do over again." But what about those who are closer in age to you? What advice would you get from those who really know what it's like being a teenager today, because they are a teenager today? We contacted a large number of "older teens" and asked them this question; *If you could go back and live your teenage years all over again, how would you approach them?* The following are a few of the many responses we received. For fun, compare their thoughts to the advice given throughout this book as well as the advice given to you by your parents and teachers.

*I would have been much kinder to the kids I thought were "nerds." I was pretty big for my age and took pleasure in "picking on" other kids. My targets were usually the "brains" and the "weaklings." Who knew that someday I'd be trying to get hired by the very same people who's lives I made difficult back when I was in school?*      – Ben Cormax, Age 19,
San Diego, CA

*I'd look deeper inside myself. Earlier in life, I looked up to many people because of their various abilities but failed to realize that those same abilities were hidden inside of me. If I had known in seventh grade that I had the potential that I discovered I had when I got to high school, I would have taken leadership positions in school much earlier. The lesson I learned here was not to be afraid to "show them," and more importantly not to be afraid to show myself what's inside!*

– Thaddeus Leopoulos, Age 19,
Little Rock, Arkansas

*I would know that the biggest role of life is attitude. It can determine anything; from grades to getting grounded. I'd know to keep smart and alert to peer pressure. I'd remember that, in any situation, my attitude determines the final outcome.*

– Amy Gudenkauf, Age 18,
Westminster, Colorado

*I would have liked to have known at a young age that if you don't "fit in" you might not be an outcast, you might just be a strong and determined person. Things like changing your hair, not seeing color, accepting those who are different, being a designated driver, showing off the fact that you are a strong believer in values and in yourself can cause quite a bit of commotion amongst high school kids. I would want to leave high school and be remembered as the girl who knew how to have a good time yet was guaranteed to make something of herself.*

– Kara Roski, Age 18,
Carmel, Indiana

*I would have gotten involved sooner. When I came to America at age thirteen from South Korea, I could not speak English. I had to concentrate very hard on learning English. As I grew up, I was surrounded by a lot of leaders, especially my friends. I envied their leadership skills. Friends told me about leadership classes and student leadership conferences. I waited for a while before joining. I never wanted to be a "normal" person who didn't care about others. I am glad I finally got involved in my school.* — Chul-Kyun Park, Age 17, San Francisco, CA

*I would go out for the school play. The guys at my school thought the play wasn't cool. I really wanted to be up on that stage, but I feared that my friends would make fun of me. So I never tried out. I was never strong enough to do my own thing. Now when I look at who my friends are, those I tried to impress are no longer around. It's a shame. I let some great chances go by because I was worried about what the other guys would say. I'll never have those opportunities again.* — William Bendix, Age 19, Long Island, NY

*I'd just "BE." We've all seen that popular cologne ad proclaiming we need to just "be" – as in "be happy" with ourselves and each other. If I was just entering my teenage years, I would "BE" more open. I know that it would lead to more meaningful friendships. To those of you who are beginning your teenage years, take advice from someone whose ending them. Life is too short for prejudice – So, just get over any biases you may have and "BE" happy!* — Merritt Finney, Age 18, Little Rock, Arkansas

*I would accept change more openly. Denying that things are going to change is the worst mistake I made as a teenager. I did not want things to change. Instead of focusing on the present which was important, I was obsessing about the past which I couldn't change. I was not welcoming change, and that nearly destroyed me. I became depressed and withdrew from almost everything.* — Uyen Nguyen, Age 17, Burnsville, Minnesota

*If I knew then what I know now, I would not sweat the small things. I'd know that "crushes" are never meant to last. I would know that artificial highs are nothing like the natural highs a healthy body can produce. I would know that smiles are the key to happiness. Most importantly, I would know that family is the most powerful relationship you will ever have.*

— Jason Vasquez, Age 19,
Hiram, OH

*I'd keep in mind that happiness is not something that can be found, but something I am responsible for creating. I'd always do my best. I would also try to remember that things are never as bad as they seem. After all, if the problems of the world were divided evenly between the people of the world, we'd all have the same number we do now.* — Tiffany Estell, Age 19,
Denver, Colorado

*I would keep learning, keep awake to amazement, and focus on being kind rather than right. I would look for opportunities rather than wait for them. I would understand that I control my own destiny and I determine what comes to pass. I would know that if I kept my attitude positive and strong, my dreams would come true. I would stand tall and proud of my beliefs, and live each day to the fullest.* — Sara Bushman, Age 19,
Wittenberg, WI